First Time Circle Time

Shared-Group Experiences for Three, Four, and Five-Year-Olds

by Cynthia Holley and Jane Walkup

Fearon Teacher Aids

Simon & Schuster Education Group

Dedication

**To Norbert, who keeps
my mind traveling.**

C.H.

**For my parents,
Ernest and Mary Frances Galloway,
who encircled my childhood with
love, wonder, and unstructured play.**

J.W.

Editorial Director: Virginia L. Murphy
Editor: Carol Williams
Copyeditor: Lisa Schwimmer
Design: Teena Remer
Illustration: Jane Walkup
Production: Rebecca Speakes

ISBN 0-86653-993-X

Printed in the United States of America

1 .9 8 7 6 5 4 3 2 1

Contents

Acknowledgments

We would like to thank the following
individuals for reviewing the material in
First Time Circle Time and sharing
their expertise:

Iris Carter, Special Educator,
Charlotte, North Carolina

Kimberly Cole, Whole Language Consultant,
Columbia, South Carolina

Sally Besaw, Media Specialist,
Charlotte-Mecklenburg Schools,
Charlotte, North Carolina

Ruth Lisenco, Educational Coordinator,
Black Forest Books

Stacy Nofsinger, Early Childhood Educator

Jeannette Davis, Director, Apple Book Company,
Charlotte, North Carolina

Constance Johnson, Speech and Language
Clinician, New York, New York

Dr. Rachel Siebert, Smith College,
Harvard School of Education

Lynne Tarleton, Early-Childhood Educator,
Charlotte, North Carolina

Introduction

First Time Circle Time is designed for teachers, teacher assistants, and other childcare professionals who are introducing group experiences to young children. It includes carefully selected activities designed to capture young children's natural interest in stories, language, and imaginative play.

While most children will be ready for simple group activities by age three, many children may not respond favorably to such structures until age four or five. There may also be some two-year-olds who show interest in short, cooperative involvements. Therefore, be flexible in the selection of activities you choose for your particular group.

Why Circle Time?

Young children need opportunities to interact and communicate with others. They need positive interaction with adults who listen and respond to them. And they need opportunities to share ideas with friends. Circle time provides a framework in which language, cognitive, and social skills can develop naturally. During circle time, children can begin to ask and answer questions; participate in songs, stories, and other forms of self-expression; and experience patience and taking turns with other children.

This teacher resource offers a rich variety of activities and materials that build on children's prior knowledge and encourages thinking, investigating, and problem solving. *First Time Circle Time* provides suggestions for ongoing opportunities to meet together in small groups, large groups, and with friends at learning centers. Because young children should be gradually introduced to structured activities in a supportive, non-threatening manner, *First Time Circle Time* offers gentle invitations for children to "come and look," "come and do," and "come and share" with others.

Why Themes?

First Time Circle Time uses themes to provide a variety of learning experiences in a way that encourages children to see how things are related to each other. Thematic teaching is based on the understanding that children learn best when information presented to them is meaningful and integrated. New information must be relevant to the child's "universe" in order for the child to make sense of it. Young children need to explore their world using all their senses—touching, tasting, smelling, hearing, and seeing. For example, a child can really learn about apples by having the opportunity to pick, hold, smell, taste, and explore many kinds of apples. Through these sensory experiences, a child will learn what an apple looks like inside, how it tastes, and what happens to an apple when it is cut open and left out over time. Such activities within any theme set the stage for a young child to learn, draw, paint, and talk about important subjects.

How to Use Circle Time Themes

The themes outlined in *First Time Circle Time* are intended to provide a focal point by which you can organize a series of learning experiences. Use circle time themes with flexibility. The activities need not be introduced in any specific sequence, but should be introduced as interest arises. A simple event, like a child bringing a caterpillar to school, can lead to a variety of extended learning experiences. Gather children together to observe the furry friend and read a story, such as *The Very Hungry Caterpillar* by Eric Carle. Choose activities and spark discussions from the theme "Clever Caterpillars" in the days that follow. How involved children become and how many days they study caterpillars will depend upon the interest generated.

Many factors will influence your choice of themes. In addition to child-initiated interests, theme selections can be influenced by seasonal occurrences, the availability of resources, and the climate and geography of your environment.

Guard against over-structuring young children. Offer planned group activities, which extend circle time topics, as optional choices. Be sensitive to the individual differences of children and recognize that certain children need to be offered quiet alternatives during group time. The role of the teacher in preschool education is one of facilitator—guiding, stimulating, and encouraging young children in developmentally appropriate activities. Plant the seeds of curiosity, then encourage young children to explore, discover, and learn with their peers in large groups, small groups, and independently.

Circle Time Format

Each theme in *First Time Circle Time* is divided into eight sections. The ideas and activities are intended to be used as a menu, not a recipe. Each section need not be introduced each day and activities can be used in any order. The needs and interests of your students will be the best indicators of which activities you include in your focus unit and the amount of time you spend with any one activity. The following activity sections are provided for each circle time theme:

Let's Look

Draw children's attention to the object or props described. This is an opportunity for children to look at the attributes of the "theme starter" and brainstorm information about what they see. Encourage children to bring related items from home as appropriate.

Let's Talk

Spark a discussion based on objects displayed in the "Let's Look" section. Encourage children to discuss and share personal experiences with respect to the items or pictures. Use open-ended questioning to encourage children to respond and stimulate their thinking. Encourage children to ask and answer questions among one another and actively participate in the discussions.

Let's Read

This section provides a bibliography of recommended picture books to share with preschoolers. The stories will help reinforce concepts introduced during circle time. Many of the stories are favorites among young children. Preschoolers need not hear a new story every day. Young children enjoy repeated readings of favorite stories. Occasionally a book may be listed in which the text is a bit too difficult for the youngest preschoolers. Adapt such books to the developmental needs of your group by rephrasing the stories into language suitable for preschoolers.

Let's Sing and Say

A collection of songs, fingerplays, poems, chants, and rhymes are provided that relate to each theme as well. Encourage children to sing along and respond with appropriate motions or rhythms. Favorite songs can be repeated over and over throughout the year.

Let's Move

In this section, children are given opportunities to build coordination through creative movement activities. These guided movement activities build social as well as physical competence.

Let's Make

These open-ended art projects are designed to stimulate creative thinking. Children will have opportunities to work in small groups and individually on projects which build upon concepts presented during circle time.

Let's Play

This section often spotlights classroom learning centers which naturally extend circle time themes. This time provides opportunities for individual and small-group independent play. You may need to show children how to use the equipment and props, but encourage self-directed play as well.

Let's Cook

A simple recipe or special snack is offered which relates to each circle time theme. Each snack can be prepared primarily by children with minimal adult assistance.

The amount of time you spend with these activities will vary from child to child and from day to day. While all children are invited to participate in circle time activities, give children opportunities to choose other options. The activities shared in this book are designed to offer choices and should be chosen and adapted to meet individual needs.

Circle Time Procedures

When planning for circle time, it is important to remember that preschoolers concentrate on whatever task is at hand. They usually do not like to leave favorite activities and generally resist interference. Periods of transition from centers to circle should be preceded by visual and auditory cues. Always provide ample time for transition so children can be prepared for change. A bell, song, or clapping signal 4 to 5 minutes before changing activities helps preschoolers "change gears."

You might want to establish a ritual for the opening and closing of circle time. Wear an apron with many pockets or a large hat with small objects attached (see "Making Props" on pages 269-270) to signal children that it is time to gather together. Or, turn down the classroom lights and turn on a lamp in the circle area. This is most effective when accompanied by soft music. Try drawing children to circle time with familiar songs, or use a song to signal the end of a circle time period.

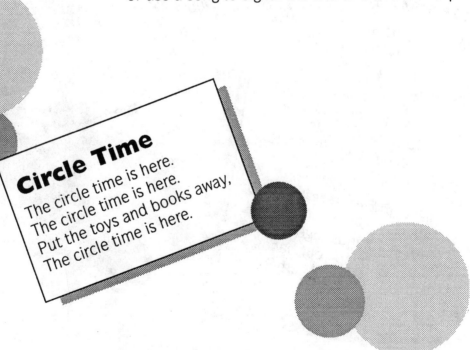

Circle Time

The circle time is here.
The circle time is here.
Put the toys and books away,
The circle time is here.

Circle Time Is Coming

(Tune: "London Bridge")

Circle time is coming now,
Coming now, coming now.
Circle time is coming now.
Let's get ready.

Put your books and toys away,
Toys away, toys away.
Put your books and toys away.
Let's get ready.

It's Time to Come to Circle

(Tune: "Did You Ever See a Lassie?")

It's time to come to circle,
To circle, to circle.
It's time to come to circle,
To circle right now.

There's Molly and Patrick
And Meggie and Jon.
(Use names of children in the classroom.)
It's time to come to circle,
To circle right now.

We're sitting in a circle,
A circle, a circle.
We're sitting in a circle,
Right here on the floor.

With Jeffrey and Sara
And Mary and Terence.
We're sitting in a circle,
Right here on the floor.

Sing a Song

Sing, sing, sing a song.
Sing a song together.
Sing, sing, sing a song.
Sing a song together.

Put your toys away.
Put your toys away.
Put your toys away.
Put your toys away.

Come, come, come to circle.
Time to come to circle.
Come, come, come to circle.
Time to come to circle.

(When all children are seated add...)
Clap, clap, clap your hands.
Clap your hands together.
Clap, clap, clap your hands.
Clap your hands together.

Closing Time Song

Open, shut them,
Open, shut them,
Give a little clap, clap, clap.
Open, shut them,
Open, shut them,
Put them in your lap, lap, lap.
Wave them, wave them,
Wave them, wave them,
High up in the sky, sky, sky.
Wave to me,
I'll wave to you.
Let's all say goodbye!

Clean-Up Time

(Tune: "London Bridge")
Now it's time to put away,
Put away, put away,
Now it's time to put away,
Our center time toys.
Take the blocks and pick them up,
Pick them up, pick them up.
Take the blocks and pick them up.
Put our toys away.

Additional Verses:
Tuck our babies in their beds ...
Put the costumes in the box ...
Put the books back on the shelf ...

Hands on Head

Hands on head.
Hands on knees.
Fold them quietly
If you please.
Look around,
Wave to a friend.
Now circle time
Is about to end!

Designing Space and Mapping Out the Room

Introducing group experiences to preschoolers involves a balance of room arrangement, props, and teacher directions. *First Time Circle Time* activities should be held in a designated place. It is important that this area include ample space for each child to sit comfortably, good lighting, and space that is free of clutter and distraction.

Seating can be determined by the shape of a rug, quilt, or sheet spread on the floor. Create a large circle on the floor, using masking tape, to define seating space. Or, laminate photographs of each child and tape them beside each child's designated place. Make movable seats using carpet squares, small cushions, pieces of foam, or plastic shapes. You may want to laminate construction-paper shapes to use as seats as well. Use shapes that are appropriate for the current theme, such as small green lily pads for the theme "Freckled Frogs."

Arrange circle areas away from learning centers and classroom traffic. If classroom space is limited, the large movement and music center can double as a circle time area. Low wooden screens or curtains can provide privacy. Try hanging a colorful golf umbrella upside down or hang fancy kites from the ceiling over the circle area. These visual cues define the space and denote fun and fantasy to the children. Puppets or other props can be brought out to introduce the circle activities. A floor lamp placed at the edge of this area can create a warm, homelike atmosphere.

A bulletin board covered with pastel shades of flannel or dark blue felt can create a focal point. Keep the pictures and shapes you use on this board simple. Portable flannel or magnetic boards are nice additions to this area as well. A record player, piano, or tape recorder can be used to invite children to the circle area. It is important for young children to see and hear the call to "come to circle time."

When arranging the learning environment for young preschoolers keep in mind the following suggestions:

1. Clearly define and mark learning centers with picture clues. Have a coding system, such as specific numbers of circles hanging over a center, to help children learn to monitor appropriate numbers of children accommodated in a particular center.

2. Interest centers should be functional—a sink near the art area, hooks in the dress-up area, shelves for books, and so on.

3. Isolate quiet centers from noisy centers. Even within centers, a cozy corner for reading or observing animals may be appropriate.

4. Traffic flow should be smooth from center to center with movement paths clear. (You wouldn't want children "passing through" the block center.) Centers should flow naturally.

5. Offer a broad range of activities within the interest centers to entertain young children's short attention spans and various maturity levels. Monitor interests and abilities as children rotate materials in and out of centers. Provide choices that lead to self-control and build self-confidence.

6. Provide storage space for children's materials as well as your own materials. Give each child his or her own cubby hole or shelf.

7. Materials should be of high quality, reflect curriculum goals, and be representative of diverse cultural backgrounds.

8. Provide space for children to display their work. The room should reflect the children and highlight their accomplishments.

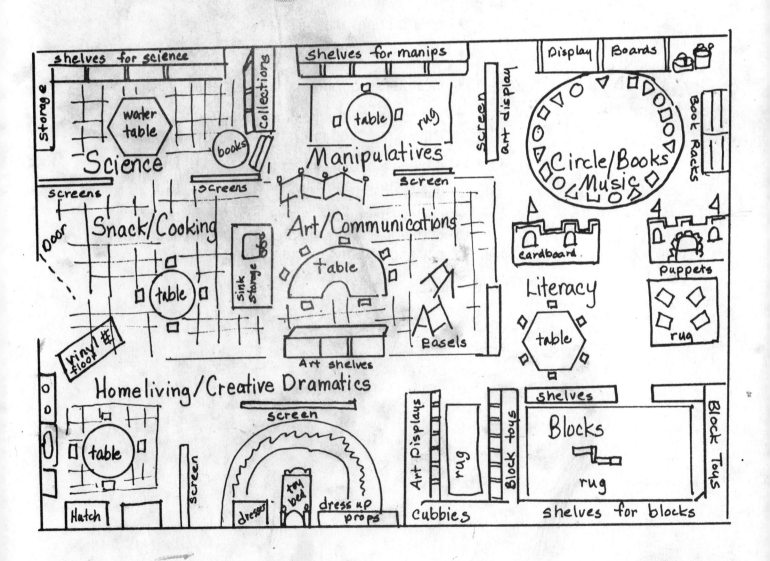

Scheduling

From Circle Time to Center Time

When scheduling the young child's day, it is important to be flexible. While routines and continuity provide security for preschoolers, rigid time schedules are intimidating and can negatively affect programming.

When scheduling programs for young children remember to

- balance active and quiet times,

- offer routines that allow flexibility,

- provide smooth transitions between tasks,

- include indoor and outdoor activities daily,

- provide opportunities for small group, large group, and individual time,

- provide a balance of structured and unstructured activities, and

- be sure to end the day on a positive note so both you and the children feel good about the day and eagerly anticipate the next.

Suggested Full-Day Schedule

7:00-8:20
Arrival and Greetings
Breakfast
Free Play at Selected
Learning Centers

8:20-8:40
Cleanup
Toileting
Toothbrushing

8:40-9:00
Morning Circle Time
- Observing
- Discussing
- Moving
- Singing
- Reading

9:00-10:00
Learning Centers
Special Art Projects

10:00-10:30
Cleanup
Toileting
Snack

10:30-11:30
Recess

11:30-11:45
Toileting

11:45-12:00
Midday Circle Time
- Fingerplays
- Stories

12:00-1:00
Lunch
Cleanup
Toileting
Toothbrushing
Quiet Activities (Music, Books)

1:00-2:30
Rest

2:30-3:30
Children Gradually Wake Up

3:30-4:30
Recess (Include Short
Teacher-Directed Movement
Activities)

4:30-4:45
Closing Circle Time
- Evaluate Day
- Songs
- Conversations
- Stories

4:45-6:00
Free Play at Selected
Learning Centers
Special Activities (Games,
Visitors)
Gradual Dismissing

Suggested Half-Day Schedule

9:00-9:15
Arrival
Table Activities

9:15-9:30
Opening Circle Time

9:30-10:30
Learning Centers

10:30-11:00
Cleanup
Toileting
Snack

11:00-11:30
Outdoor Play

11:30-11:45
Toileting
Transitional Activities
(Fingerplays, Songs)

11:45-12:00
Closing Circle Time

12:00
Dismissal

Circle Time Themes

Magnificent Me

Young children are the center of their own universe. They are very interested in their bodies and how they work. The themes in this section are designed to help children appreciate their bodies and explore ways they can move.

Fabulous Faces

Let's Look

Display pictures of various faces. Encourage children to identify parts of the faces and guess who the people might be.

Pass around a hand mirror so children can take turns looking at their own faces.

Take photographs of students to play the "mystery child" game. Cover a photograph with construction paper. Gradually tear away the construction paper until children can guess who is in the picture.

Let's Talk

- Where is your face?

- Where are your eyes, nose, and ears?

- What can you make your face do? Can you make your face cry? Laugh? Smile? Blink? Wink?

- How do you look when you are sad? Happy? Angry? Surprised? Scared?

- Does your face look the same as other faces you see?

- How are faces different from each other?

Let's Read

Bodies by Barbara Brenner

Bright Eyes, Brown Skin by Cheryl Willis Hudson and Bernette G. Ford

Daydreamers by Eloise Greenfield

Faces by Barbara Brenner

Grandpa's Face by Eloise Greenfield

The Important Book by Margaret Wise Brown

Nathan's Day by Susan Conlin

On Monday When It Rained by Cherryl Kachenmeister

Someone Special Just Like You by Tricia Brown

Sometimes I Like to Cry by Elizabeth and Henry Stanton

Let's Sing and Say

Eye Winker

Eye winker,
(Point to eyes.)
Tom Tinker,
(Point to ears.)
Nose smeller,
(Point to nose.)
Mouth eater,
(Point to mouth.)
Chin chopper,
(Point to chin.)
Chin chopper,
chin chopper,
chin chopper, chin!

Touch My Hair

I touch my hair, my lips, my eyes.
(Children touch hair, lips, and eyes.)
I sit up straight, then I rise.
(Sit up straight and then stand up.)
I touch my eyes, my nose, my chin.
(Touch eyes, nose, and chin.)
And then I sit back down again.
(Sit down.)

Two Little Eyes

Two little eyes
that open and close.
(Point to eyes.)
Two little ears
and one little nose.
(Point to ears and nose.)
Two little cheeks
and one little chin.
(Point to cheeks and chin.)
Two little lips
with the teeth closed in!
(Point to lips and teeth.)

Who Feels Happy?

Who feels happy? Who wants to say?
All who do clap their hands this way
(clap, clap).
Who feels happy? Who wants to say?
All who do nod their heads this way
(nod, nod).
Who feels happy? Who wants to say?
All who do stamp your feet this way
(stamp, stamp).
Who feels happy? Who wants to say?
All who do wave their hands this way
(wave, wave).
Who feels happy? Who wants to say?
All who do tap their shoulders this way
(tap, tap).

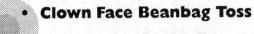

Let's Move

• Clown Face Beanbag Toss

Draw a clown face on a large cardboard box. Draw and cut out large circles for the eyes, nose, and mouth. Invite children to toss beanbags through the holes.

• The Moving Game

Encourage children to move freely as you suggest movement ideas. Challenge children to move like frightened mice, sleepy cats, hungry lions, happy butterflies, tired babies, and so on. Invite children to think of their own movement ideas as they express emotions and feelings with their faces and bodies.

Let's Make

• Self Portraits

- drawing paper

- pencils

- tempera paint or watercolors

- paintbrushes

Encourage children to draw or paint a picture of themselves. Accept each child's picture based on his or her developmental level. Save these portraits and compare them with portraits made by the children later in the year.

• Framed Faces

- polaroid camera

- cardboard

- scissors

- glue
- collage materials, such as sequins, shells, buttons, and ribbon

Take a polaroid picture of each child. Cut cardboard frames to fit around each photograph. Glue the photographs to the frames. Or, you may wish to glue the photographs to squares of cardboard, leaving approximately an inch around the edges for a frame. Invite children to decorate their picture frames with collage materials. These make nice gifts.

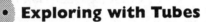

Let's Play

Exploring with Tubes

Props: cardboard tubes

Give each child a cardboard tube to take along on a "discovery walk." Stop at a quiet location on the school grounds and invite children to choose one spot to carefully examine. Encourage children to observe their chosen spots by looking through their cardboard tubes. Children can also put the tubes to their ears and describe the sounds they hear.

Aroma Art

Props: easel paints and brushes, drawing paper, spices, and extracts

Add cinnamon, cloves, or peppermint extract to easel paints. Invite children to create colorful pictures with interesting smells.

Eye Spy

Props: kaleidoscopes, octascopes, binoculars, periscopes, and sunglasses

Display a variety of interesting eyewear and viewing aids. Invite children to freely use the materials, exploring the things they see using the props.

Water Scopes

Props: plastic drink bottle filled with orange water and a drop of dishwashing detergent, another bottle filled with blue water and a tablespoon of cooking oil, a third bottle filled with water and pieces of colored cellophane, and a fourth bottle filled with water and curling ribbon or marbles

Be sure the cap on each bottle is securely tightened. For safety reasons, place book tape around each cap. Invite children to shake the bottles and hold them up to the light to view interesting designs and patterns.

Let's Cook

Gingerbread Faces

- 1 cup shortening
- 1 cup brown sugar
- 3 eggs
- 2 cups molasses
- 8 cups flour
- 2 tsp soda
- 1/2 tsp ginger
- 1 Tbsp cinnamon
- raisins
- sunflower seeds

Invite children to help measure and mix the ingredients (or you can use a gingerbread box mix). Cream together the sugar and shortening. Add the eggs and molasses and mix well. Sift the dry ingredients in a separate bowl. Add to the mixture and stir well. Refrigerate the mixture until cold. Roll the dough out on a lightly floured cutting board to a 1/2" thickness. Using a cookie cutter, invite each child to cut a round gingerbread face from the dough. Children can use raisins and sunflower seeds to add facial features. Place the gingerbread faces on a cookie sheet and bake at 375° F for 8 to 10 minutes.

Holding Hands

Let's Look

Put a pair of mittens on your ears, nose, and head and see how children respond. Display a tray with nail polish, nail clippers, emery boards, rings, and hand cream for children to identify.

Let's Talk

- What can you do with your hands? Can you wave? Clap? Snap?

- What else can you wear on your hands besides mittens?

- Why do people wear mittens?

- Why do people wear nail polish, rings, and gloves?

- Do you know what this is for? (Point to each object.)

Let's Read

Here Are My Hands by Bill Martin, Jr.

I Touch by Rachel Isadora

The Mitten by Alvin Tresselt

Mitten Kitten by Jerome Martin

My Hands Can by Jean Holzenthaler

Let's Sing and Say

Let Your Hands Go Clap

Let your hands go clap, clap, clap.
(Clap hands.)
Let your fingers tap, tap, tap.
(Tap fingers.)
Roll your hands around and 'round,
(Roll hands one over the other.)
And lay them quietly right down.
(Lay hands in lap.)

Open Them, Shut Them

Open them, shut them,
open them, shut them,
(Open and close hands.)
Give a little clap, clap, clap.
(Clap hands.)
Open them, shut them,
open them, shut them,
(Open and close hands.)
Put them in your lap, lap, lap.
(Place hands in lap.)
Creep them, creep them,
creep them, creep them,
(Creep hand up the other arm.)
Right up to your
chin, chin, chin.
(Tap chin.)
Open up your little mouth
but do not let them in, in, in!
(Open mouth and then touch the outside of mouth.)

Where Is Thumbkin?

(Tune: "Are You Sleeping?")
Where is Thumbkin?
Where is Thumbkin?
Here I am, here I am.
(Hold up each thumb.)
How are you today, sir?
(Wiggle thumbs.)
Very well, I thank you!
Run away, run away!
(Run thumbs behind back.)

(Repeat with the other fingers.)
Where is Pointer...
Where is Tall Man...
Where is Ringer...
Where is Pinky...

My Hands

My hands upon my head I place.
On my shoulders, on my face.
Now I raise them up so high,
Make my fingers quickly fly.
Now I clap them, one, two, three.
Then I fold them silently.
(Children imitate directions.)

Let's Move

● Throw and Catch

Encourage children to throw and catch beanbags and various balls (beach balls, tennis balls, soft sponge balls, and small plastic golf balls). Challenge children to throw the balls without using their hands.

Let's Make

• Clay Creations

- large tub of clay

- plastic combs

- popsicle sticks

- plastic knives and forks

- hair rollers

Place a large tub of clay (see recipe for clay #2 on page 268) on a low table. Invite children to pinch off small balls of clay and explore the clay's texture and pliability. Encourage children to touch the clay with their hands, fists, and elbows. Then introduce a few simple implements for carving and molding, such as those listed here.

• Festive Fingerpaint Prints

- plastic or styrofoam trays (one per child)

- liquid starch

- food coloring

- eyedroppers

- glitter, paper confetti, cornmeal, salt, or sand

Pour a spoonful of liquid starch on a plastic or styrofoam tray for each child. Invite each child to add drops of food coloring to the starch. Encourage children to fingerpaint with the colored starch by spreading it around on the tray. Add glitter, paper confetti, cornmeal, salt, or sand to the wet starch paint to create interesting textures. Let the trays dry thoroughly and display in the classroom.

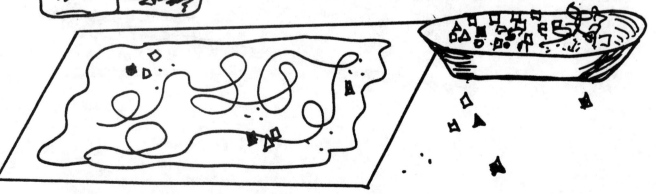

Let's Play

Mitten Match

Props: mittens, gloves, clothesline, and clothespins

Hang a clothesline across your classroom. Invite children to match pairs of mittens and gloves and then use clothespins to hang them together on the line.

Manicure Stand

Props: emery boards, nail buffers, pretend nail polish (colored water), cotton balls, small dish of soapy water, hand lotion, small table and two chairs, appointment book, and "open" and "closed" signs

Invite children to role-play being manicurists, receptionists, or customers using the appropriate props.

Let's Cook

Cheesy Roll-Ups

- wheat bread (1 slice per child)
- 8 oz cream cheese
- 4 oz crushed pineapple, drained
- plastic knives

Cut the crusts off the slices of bread. Give each child a slice of bread and have children press the bread flat with their hands. Then mix the cream cheese and pineapple together. Help children spread the mixture on the bread and then roll the bread into logs. Cut the children's rolls into six pieces to make finger snacks.

Hats on Heads

Let's Look

Wear a hat to school and bring various other hats for children to explore. Invite children to sort the hats by color, size, and type. Plan a special "hat day" and encourage students to wear a special hat to school.

Let's Talk

- What do you wear on your head?

- What do you wear when it rains? Snows?

- Why do we wear clothes?

- Why are hats important? Do you think it's important to wear a hat when it's cold outside? Why?

Let's Read

Animals Should Definitely Not Wear Clothing by Judi Barrett

Aunt Flossie's Hats by Elizabeth Fitzgerald Howard

Caps for Sale by Esphyr Slobodkina

Caps, Hats, Socks, and Mittens by Louise Borden

Hats, Hats, Hats by Ann Morris

Ho for a Hat! by Jay Smith

Mister Momboo's Hat by Ralph Leemis

Whose Hat Is That? by Ron Roy

Whose Hat? by Margaret Miller

Let's Sing and Say

The Three-Cornered Hat

My hat it has three corners,
Three corners has my hat.
A hat without three corners
Could never be my hat.

My Tall Silk Hat

One day I took a ride upon the subway,
My tall silk hat, my tall silk hat!
I went to put it on the seat beside me,
My tall silk hat, my tall silk hat!
A lady came and sat upon it,
My tall silk hat, she squashed it flat!
And then a lady sat upon it,
My tall silk hat, it looked like that!
Goodness gracious,
now what do you think of that?
A lady sat upon my hat!
Upon my hat, upon my hat!
Oh yes, she sat upon my hat!
Tell me everybody,
now what do you think of that?
(Imitate appropriate movements.)

Head, Shoulders, Knees, and Toes

My head, my shoulders,
my knees, my toes.
My head, my shoulders,
my knees, my toes.
My head, my shoulders,
my knees, my toes.
My head, my shoulders,
my knees, my toes.
Let's all clap hands together
(clap, clap).
(Children touch parts as named.
Other parts can be
interchanged—eyes, nose,
fingers, ears—as desired.)

Let's Move

- **Hats Off**

Play "Follow the Leader" to music with the children.
One child begins as the leader and wears the
"leader hat." Play music as the leader starts a
motion and the other children imitate. When the
leader takes off his or her hat, everyone must
freeze and the music stops. When the leader
replaces his or her hat, the music begins again
and everyone continues.

Let's Make

Happy Hats

- styrofoam plates (one per child)
- scissors
- glue colored with food coloring
- paper scraps
- cotton balls
- ribbon and sequins or shiny beads
- plastic and paper flowers

Cut the center out of a styrofoam plate for each child. Cut through the remaining rings so that the hats can be adjusted to each child's head. Invite children to spread the colored glue on their hats and add paper scraps, cotton balls, ribbon, sequins, beads, and flowers for decoration.

Painter's Hat

- paper painter's hats
- markers

Inexpensive paper painter's hats can be purchased at most hardware stores. Invite each child to decorate his or her own hat using different-colored markers.

Visors

- styrofoam plates
- scissors
- star stickers and markers
- stapler and elastic

Give each child a styrofoam plate. Help the children cut the plates in crescent shapes to make visors. Invite children to decorate their visors using markers and star stickers. Staple a piece of elastic to each side of the visors to fit across the back of the children's heads.

Let's Play

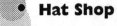

Hat Shop

Props: variety of hats (visors, caps, headbands), full-length mirror, large paper bags, play money, and cash register

Encourage some children to role-play customers in a hat shop by trying on and then "buying" their special hats. Invite other children to role-play store clerks to make change and put the purchases in paper bags for the customers.

Let's Cook

Toppers

- wheat bread (2 slices per child)
- cheese spread
- chopped olives
- raisins
- sunflower seeds
- cookie cutters
- plastic knives

Help children cut several small hat shapes from the bread using cookie cutters. Invite children to spread each hat shape with cheese spread and then sprinkle olives, raisins, and sunflower seeds on top of their bread shapes to decorate the sandwiches. Enjoy the toppers as a healthy snack.

Fancy Feet

Let's Look

Fill a box with a variety of shoes, such as tennis shoes, loafers, slippers, boots, thongs, galoshes, sandals, and so on. Or, bring in pictures of a variety of footwear. Point out the differences in size, shape, and style of the different shoes. Then invite children to take off their shoes and socks and count their toes.

Let's Talk

- What can you do with your feet? (Demonstrate walking, running, hopping, and jumping.)

- What can you wear on your feet?

- Why do you wear shoes? When do you wear boots? Sandals? Sneakers?

- Are your feet ticklish?

Let's Read

My Feet by Aliki

Shoes by Elizabeth Winthrop

Shoes from Grandpa by Mem Fox

The Snowy Day by Ezra Jack Keats

Two New Sneakers by Nancy Tafuri

Whose Shoes Are These? by Ron Roy

Whose Shoes? by Brian Wildsmith

Whose Shoes? by Margaret Miller

Let's Sing and Say

Five Toes
This little pig went to market.
This little pig stayed at home.
This little pig had roast beef.
This little pig had none.
This little pig said, "Wee, wee!
I can't find my way home."

Let Everyone Clap Hands with Me
Let everyone clap hands with me (clap, clap).
It's easy as easy can be (clap, clap).
Come on in and join in the game (clap, clap).
Just watch me and you do the same (clap, clap).
Clap hands, clap and be merry,
Clap hands, clap them again.
Clap hands, clap and be merry.
Clap till the walls start to shake (clap, clap).
Clap till the walls start to shake (clap, clap).

Additional Verses:
Let everyone stomp feet with me (stomp, stomp).
Let everyone slap knees with me (slap, slap).
Let everyone shout out "Yoo-hoo" ("Yoo-hoo!")!
Let everyone whisper "Yoo-hoo" ("Yoo-hoo").

Two Little Hands Go Clap, Clap, Clap
Two little hands go clap, clap, clap.
Two little feet go tap, tap, tap.
One little body turns around
And sits quietly right down.
(Imitate designated movements.)

Cobbler, Cobbler
Cobbler, cobbler, mend my shoe.
(Hold one foot across the other knee.)
Have it done by half-past two.
(Hammer shoe with fist.)
Stitch it up and stitch it down.
(Imitate a sewing motion.)
Now nail the heel all around.
(Hammer the heel of shoe with fist.)

Let's Move

• Fun Feet

Invite children to explore how many ways their feet can move. Encourage children to hop on one foot and then the other, balance on one foot, walk heel to toe, walk side to side, gallop, march, and so on.

• Texture Walks

Bring in a large box and a variety of material, such as sand, rice, or mud. Place the materials in the box, one at a time, and invite children to walk in the box of sand, rice, or mud without their shoes!

• Sort Shoes

Have each child take off one shoe. Put all the shoes in a pile. Then invite children to find their missing shoes.

Let's Make

Footprints

- tempera paint
- shallow tray or pan
- butcher paper
- bucket of soapy water

Place tempera paint in a shallow tray or pan. Place a long, narrow piece of butcher paper on the floor by the pan. Then invite children to carefully dip their bare feet in the paint and walk across the butcher paper to make colorful footprints. Help children rinse their feet in a bucket of soapy water at the end of the footprint walk. Hang the completed work on the ceiling or a wall.

Tennis-Shoe Rubbings

- newsprint
- tape
- chalk or crayons

Cut newsprint into rectangles slightly larger than a child's shoe. Tape a paper rectangle around the sole of each child's shoe. Invite children to use chalk or crayons to rub over the newsprint on the bottom of their shoes to capture the shoe's textured design.

Shoe Prints

- sand
- water
- shallow tray or pan
- plaster of Paris

Place the sand in a shallow tray or pan. Dampen the sand with water. Then invite children to step in the wet sand to make shoe prints. Pour plaster of Paris into the wet shoe prints. After the plaster has hardened, remove the prints.

Let's Play

Lacers

Props: big boots with laces, lacing boards, and shoelaces

To make a lacing board, cut a boot shape from tagboard and punch holes in it. Invite children to practice lacing and tying the shoelaces on the boots or lacing boards.

The Spit-Spot Shoeshine Shop

Props: several pairs of leather shoes, saddle soap (non-toxic), shoe rags, brushes, and buffers

Demonstrate how to apply shoe polish to the shoes and then buff the shoes. Invite children to continue this activity during independent time.

Let's Cook

Hoppin' Good Drinks

- frozen fruit yogurt
- milk
- sturdy plastic jars with lids or junior baby food jars

Place one tablespoon of frozen yogurt and 1/2 cup of milk in a jar for each child. Have each child secure the lid of his or her jar and then hold the jar tightly in both hands. Invite children to mix their drinks by carefully shaking their jars. When mixed, pour the drinks into cups and enjoy.

Circle Time Themes

Playful Pets

While children may be in awe of large animals, they also delight in observing and studying creatures smaller than themselves. These themes provide a chance for children to observe the habits of classroom pets or animal guests and learn how to properly care for them.

Cunning Cats

Let's Look

Invite someone to bring a cat or kittens to visit your class during circle time. If this is not possible, display pictures of cats. Glue a cat picture inside a colorful file folder. Cut several doors or windows out of the folder flap that covers the picture. Open one door at a time and invite children to guess what animal picture is hidden inside.

Let's Talk

- Who has a cat for a pet?

- How does a kitten feel?

- Can a tiger be a pet?

- What do tigers eat?

- How do kittens sound?

- How do tigers sound?

Let's Read

Angus and the Cat by Marjorie Flack

Cat Goes Fiddle-I-Fee by Paul Galdone

Cats Do, Dogs Don't by Norma Simon

The Farmyard Cat by Christine Anello

Have You Seen My Cat? by Eric Carle

Here Comes the Cat! by Frank Asch

Millions of Cats by Wanda Gag

One Little Kitten by Tana Hoban

Pretend You're a Cat by Jean Marzollo

Three Little Kittens by Paul Galdone

Pussy Cat and Queen

"Pussy cat, pussy cat,
Where have you been?"
"I've been to London
To see the Queen."
"Pussy cat, pussy cat,
What did you there?"
"I frightened a little mouse
under the chair."

I Love Little Kitty

I love little kitty, her coat is so warm,
And if I don't hurt her, she'll do me no harm.
So I'll not pull her tail nor drive her away,
But kitty and I very gently will play.
She shall sit by my side,
and I'll give her some food.
And kitty will love me because I am good.

Let's Sing and Say

Kitten Is Hiding

A kitten is hiding under a chair,
(Hide one thumb under the other hand.)
I looked and looked for him everywhere,
(Hold hand across eyebrows, looking.)
Under the table and under the bed;
(Keep looking around.)
I looked in the corner, and when I said,
"Come Kitty, come Kitty, here's milk for you,"
(Hold out cupped hands.)
Kitty came running and calling, "Mew, mew."
(Run the fingers of one hand up other arm.)

Let's Move

• Alley Cat

Invite children to pretend they are cats. Children can walk like cats, arch up with their backs, pounce, pretend they are cats playing with balls of string, or curl up like cats in the sun. Play a recording of "Alley Cat." Encourage children to dance freely to the music.

Let's Make

• Cat Costumes

- black and gray construction paper
- scissors
- washable markers or eyebrow pencils
- yarn
- safety pins
- stapler

Cut construction paper into 3" x 18" strips and a variety of triangular and circular shapes. Invite each child to glue two ear shapes to a strip to make an ear headband. Carefully staple the finished headbands around each child's head. Help children use washable markers or eyebrow pencils to draw whiskers on their faces. Use safety pins to attach yarn tails to their clothing.

Kitty Cat Yarn Designs

- diluted glue in paper cups

- yarn

- construction paper (dark colors)

Give each child a sheet of dark construction paper and several pieces of yarn in a variety of colors and sizes. Invite children to dip the yarn in the glue and place the yarn on the colored paper to make creative designs.

• •

Let's Play

Cat's Playground

Props: climb-through barrel, inclined planes, big balls, and a hanging yarn ball

Ask children what they think cats like to play with. Use their suggestions to set up a "cat" obstacle course. Invite children to maneuver through the course. Encourage children to demonstrate cat-like movements, such as batting the hanging yarn ball with their "claws."

Cats to the Vet

Props: examining table, phone, appointment book, tongue depressors, splints, strips of cloth, wide masking tape, cotton balls, gauze, boxes, doctor's kit, clipboards, and paper

Set up a veterinarian's office in your room. Use boxes to create animal cages and an x-ray machine. Encourage children to use the props in ways they think a veterinarian might. For example, children can attach a clipboard to each "cage" for the "patient's" chart. Invite children to bring stuffed toy cats and other animals from home as well.

Let's Cook

Kitty's Warm Milk

- low-fat milk
- bowls
- plastic spoons
- nutmeg and cinnamon

Heat a panful of milk until it is just warm (not hot). Pour a small amount into a bowl for each child. Invite children to sprinkle nutmeg and cinnamon over the warm milk. Then join the children in lapping up the milk with a spoon!

Mischievous Mice

Let's Look

Use a mouse puppet to welcome children to circle time. Ask someone to bring in a pet mouse or borrow a small mouse from a pet store to show children. If a real mouse is not available, display pictures of mice. Point out some mice features, such as a long tail, furry body, and whiskers.

Let's Talk

- Does anyone have a pet like this?

- Is it big or little?

- Can you play with mice? Why or why not?

- What safety rules should you remember about mice?

- What do mice eat?

Let's Read

Alexander and the Wind-Up Mouse by Leo Lionni

At Mary Bloom's by Aliki

If You Give a Mouse a Cookie by Laura Jaffe Numeroff

Mouse Around by Pat Schories

Mouse Count by Ellen S. Walsh

Mouse Paint by Ellen S. Walsh

Two Tiny Mice by Alan Baker

Under the Moon by Joanne Ryder

Whose Mouse Are You? by Robert Kraus

Let's Sing and Say

Three Blind Mice

Three blind mice! Three blind mice!
See how they run! See how they run!
They all ran after the farmer's wife,
She tickled their tails with a butter knife.
Did you ever see such a sight in your life,
As three blind mice?

Hickory Dickory Dock

Hickory dickory dock.
The mouse ran up the clock.
The clock struck one.
The mouse ran down,
Hickory dickory dock. TICK, TOCK!

Five Little Mice

Five little mice on the pantry floor,
(Hold up five fingers.)
This little mouse peeked behind the door,
(Bend down little finger.)
This little mouse nibbled at the cake,
(Bend down ring finger.)
This little mouse not a sound did make,
(Bend down middle finger.)
This little mouse took a bite of cheese,
(Bend down index finger.)
This little mouse heard a kitten sneeze.
(Bend down thumb.)
"Ah-choo," sneezed the kitten,
And "Squeak," they cried,
(Imitate sneezing and being startled.)
As they found a hole and ran inside.
*(Put hand on opposite hip, making a hole with
fingers, and run the other fingers through the hole.)*

The Old Gray Cat

The old gray cat is sleeping, sleeping, sleeping,
The old gray cat is sleeping in the house.
The little mice come creeping, creeping, creeping,
The little mice come creeping in the house.
The little mice are nibbling, nibbling, nibbling,
The little mice come nibbling in the house.
The old gray cat comes sneaking, sneaking, sneaking,
The old gray cat comes sneaking in the house.
The little mice all scamper, scamper, scamper,
The little mice all scamper from the house!
*(Imitate appropriate motions of sleeping, creeping, nib-
bling, sneaking, and scampering for each verse.)*

Let's Move

• Sneaky Mice

Invite children to pretend to be mice hiding in a little hole behind the kitchen wall. Encourage children to peek out of the hole and look around. Children can carefully sneak out of the hole and scamper around the room. Instruct children to stop when you say "Here comes the old Tom cat!" and then run back to the safety of their holes. Repeat several times.

Let's Make

• Swiss Cheese

- playdough

- food coloring

- plastic straws, chopsticks, or popsicle sticks

Prepare a batch of playdough (see recipe for playdough on page 267). Invite children to pull off pieces of the playdough and poke holes in the playdough to make Swiss cheese. Add yellow or orange food coloring to the playdough, if you wish. Display the children's cheesy creations on a table, or store the playdough for another day.

• Mouse Colors

- *Mouse Paint* by Ellen S. Walsh

- paper cups filled with colored water

- tray

- eyedroppers

- tissue paper, coffee filters, facial tissues, and paper towels

After reading the book *Mouse Paint*, place cups of colored water on a tray. Give each child an eyedropper and a selection of tissue paper, coffee filters, facial tissue, and paper towels. Show the children how to use the eyedroppers to squeeze droplets of colored water onto the papers. Encourage children to notice and compare the differences in how colors spread on the various types of paper.

Let's Play

Mouse House

Props: cardboard mouse hole, mouse ear headbands, and toy cheese

Cut a large piece of cardboard to look like the opening to a mouse hole. Place the mouse hole in front of the door to the housekeeping center or other learning center. Encourage children to pretend they are mice and creep and crawl through the mouse hole and pretend to eat cheese.

Crawling Mice

Props: masking tape maze

Using masking tape, outline a mouse maze on your classroom floor. Invite children to pretend to be mice and crawl through the maze.

Let's Cook

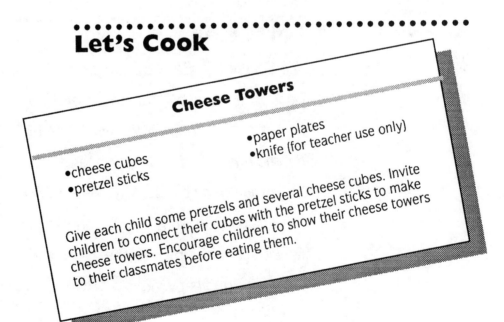

Cheese Towers

- cheese cubes
- pretzel sticks
- paper plates
- knife (for teacher use only)

Give each child some pretzels and several cheese cubes. Invite children to connect their cubes with the pretzel sticks to make cheese towers. Encourage children to show their cheese towers to their classmates before eating them.

Beautiful Bunnies

Let's Look

Invite children to bring in all types of toy rabbits and bunnies they may have at home. Display the rabbits in the circle area. If possible, borrow a pet rabbit from a pet store or friend for children to observe.

Let's Talk

- What do rabbits look like?
- How do rabbits sound?
- How do rabbits move?
- How do rabbits feel when you touch them?
- How are rabbits different from other small, furry animals?
- How are our collection of toy rabbits alike?

Let's Read

The Golden Egg Book by Margaret Wise Brown

Goodnight Moon by Margaret Wise Brown

Ho Lim Lim: A Rabbit Tale from Japan by Tejima

Pat the Bunny by Dorothy Kunhardt

Runaway Bunny by Margaret Wise Brown

The Tale of Peter Rabbit by Beatrix Potter

Ten Little Bunnies by Marlene E. Gawron

Ten Little Rabbits by Virginia Grossman and Sylvia Long

Little Bunny Foo Foo

Little Bunny Foo Foo,
Hopping through the forest.
(Raise two fingers and "hop" hand through the air.)
Scooping up the field mice,
(Scoop cupped hand in the air.)
And tickling them on the head!
("Tickle" fist of one hand in palm of other hand.)
Down came the good fairy and said,
"Little Bunny Foo Foo,
I don't like your attitude—
(Shake a finger as if scolding Bunny.)
Scooping up field mice
(Scoop cupped hand in the air.)
And tickling them on the head.
("Tickle" fist of one hand in palm of other hand.)
I'll give you three chances
And if you don't behave,
(Shake a finger as if scolding Bunny.)
I'll turn you into a goon!"

And on the next day came
Little Bunny Foo Foo,
Hopping through the forest...
(Repeat as above for "two chances" and "one more chance.")
And on the fourth day came
Little Bunny Foo Foo,
Hopping through the forest.
(Raise two fingers and "hop" hand through the air.)
Scooping up the field mice,
(Scoop cupped hand in the air.)
And tickling them on the head!
("Tickle" fist of one hand in palm of other hand.)
Down came the good fairy for the last time and said,
"Little Bunny Foo Foo,
I gave you three chances
And you still didn't behave.
(Shake a finger as if scolding Bunny.)
Now I'll turn you into a goon!"
POOF!
(Hold up both fists and quickly open them.)

(Young children enjoy this verse for its motions even though they may not understand its moral: Hare today and goon tomorrow.)

Bunny

Here is bunny
with ears so funny.
(Hold up first two fingers, slightly bent.)
And here is a
hole in the ground.
(Place hand on hip forming an opening with arm.)
When a noise he hears,
he pricks up his ears,
(Quickly straighten first two fingers.)
And he jumps in the hole
with a bound!
(Jump hand like a bunny through the opening.)

Five Little Rabbits

Five little rabbits sitting by the door—
One hopped away, and then there were four.

Refrain:
Hop, hop, hop, hop.
See how they run.
Hop, hop, hop, hop.
They think it's great fun.

Four little rabbits under a tree—
One hopped away, and then there were three.
(Repeat refrain.)

Three little rabbits looking at you—
One hopped away, and then there were two.
(Repeat refrain.)

Two little rabbits resting in the sun—
One hopped away, and then there was one.
(Repeat refrain.)

One little rabbit left all alone—
He hopped away and then there were none.
(Repeat refrain.)

(Hold up the appropriate number of fingers for each verse. For refrain, hold up two fingers and hop with hand like a bunny.)

Let's Move

Bunny Hops

Invite children to pretend to be bunnies. "Bunnies" can hop, pause on back legs to listen, twitch their bunny ears, shake their bunny tails, and wiggle their bunny noses. Finally, children can hop back to the burrow to curl up and sleep.

Let's Make

Carrot Prints

- carrots

- knife (for teacher use only)

- nail (for teacher use only)

- tempera paint (orange and yellow)

- newspaper

Cut off the top of each carrot. Use the carrot tops for printmaking and save the rest of the carrots for a snack. Give each child one carrot top. Encourage children to think of a simple design for their carrot prints. Carve designs in the ends of the carrots, listening carefully as each child gives you directions. Then invite children to dip the carrot ends in tempera paint and make prints on newspaper.

- **Rabbit-Tail Prints**

- spray bottles

- drawing paper

- powdered tempera paint in shallow bowls

- cotton balls

- clothespins

Attach cotton balls to the ends of clothespins to make "rabbit-tail" paintbrushes. Place several rabbit-tail brushes and bowls of powdered tempera paint on a table. Give each child a small spray bottle filled with water and a large piece of drawing paper. Help children spray their drawing papers with water. Then invite children to dip rabbit-tail brushes in the dry paint and spread the paint on the wet papers.

Let's Play

• Hopping Down the Bunny Trail

Props: hopping trail marked with masking tape, large cardboard box, and books about rabbits

Tape X's around the circle time area in an interesting hopping pattern. Place some X's close together and some farther apart. Wind the trail around so children can follow it to a large cardboard box with a hole cut in it for a burrow. Place some rabbit books in the burrow for children to read or look at. Invite children to hop on one foot or two as they follow the X's to the burrow.

• Rabbit Patch Pull

Props: paper carrots with paper clips attached, cardboard box, magnets, and yarn or string

Cut carrots from orange construction paper and laminate both sides. Or, cover the paper carrots with clear contact paper. Place paper clips on the end of each carrot top. Hide the carrots in a cardboard box. Tie a magnet to the end of each piece of yarn or string. Invite children to pretend to be bunnies "catching carrots." Children can hang the magnet ends of the strings down into the cardboard box. The magnets will attract the paper clips and students can pull up their carrot catches.

Let's Cook

Rabbit Food

- carrots (with tops, if available)
- celery
- knife (for teacher use only)
- fruit-flavored yogurt
- tray
- small bowls
- vegetable peeler

Invite children to help wash the vegetables. Peel and slice the vegetables and arrange them on a tray. Give each child a small bowl of fruit-flavored yogurt. Encourage children to dip the vegetables in the yogurt before eating them.

Fantastic Fish

Let's Look

Bring a bowl of goldfish to circle time. Encourage children to notice the colors, shapes, and movements of the fish. Display pictures of a variety of fish. If possible, use a fishing pole, net, and tackle box to demonstrate how to catch a fish.

Let's Talk

- How are fish alike? How are they different?

- Where do fish live?

- What do fish eat?

- How do fish breathe?

- Are fish dangerous?

- What would you do if you saw a shark while swimming?

- How can you catch fish?

- Have you ever gone fishing?

Let's Read

Big Al by Andrew Clements

Fish Eyes: A Book You Can Count On by Lois Ehlert

Fish Is Fish by Leo Lionni

Five Silly Fisherman by Roberta Edwards

Gone Fishing by Earlene R. Long

Gone Fishing by Steven Kroll

Just Like Daddy by Frank Asch

Swimmy by Leo Lionni

Let's Sing and Say

I Caught a Fish Alive

One, two, three, four, five,
(Hold up five fingers,
one at a time.)
I caught a fish alive.
(Imitate holding up a fish.)
Six, seven, eight, nine, ten,
(Raise the fingers of other hand.)
I let it go again.
(Imitate throwing the fish back.)
Why did I let it go?
(Hold up hands, looking puzzled.)
Because it bit my finger so!
(Shake right hand.)
Which finger did it bite?
(Hold up right hand.)
The little finger on the right.
(Hold up little finger.)

Catch a Fish

(Tune: "Row, Row, Row Your Boat")
Catch, catch, catch a fish,
Hook it on your line.
Reel it, reel it, reel it, reel it,
This one will be mine.

Golden Fishes

Golden fishes swimming, floating,
Swimming, floating all the day,
Golden fishes in a school they travel,
Down in the ocean and down by the bay.
(Hold the palms of hands together,
imitating swimming fish.)

Did You Ever Go Fishing?

Did you ever go fishing on a bright sunny day,
Sit on a fence and have the fence give way,
Slide off the fence and rip your pants,
And see the little fishes do the
hootchy-kootchy dance?

Let's Move

Sea Creatures

Invite children to pretend to swim like fish, walk like crabs, or crawl like starfish.

Let's Make

Fishing Kits

- sticks (yardsticks, meter sticks, or dowels)

- string

- paper clips

- egg cartons

- rubber worms

- pipe cleaners

Help the children tie string to sticks to make fishing poles. Attach paper clips to one end of the fishing lines for hooks. Add pipe-cleaner handles to egg cartons for tackle boxes. Fill the tackle boxes with rubber worms. Then invite the children to pretend to go fishing.

Worm Mural

- fishing pole (or string attached to a stick)

- rubber worms

- butcher paper

- tempera paint

Attach rubber worms to the ends of fishing lines. (Use the fishing kits from the previous activity.) Invite children to dip the worms in tempera paint and then dangle them on butcher paper to make interesting worm designs.

Let's Play

Seashell Match-Up

Props: seashells and construction-paper seashell mat

Select eight small shells of different shapes to make a seashell matching game. Trace each shell shape onto light-colored construction paper. Outline the shells with a dark marker. Cut out the shell shapes and glue them to a piece of dark construction paper to make a seashell mat. Laminate the seashell mat or cover it with clear contact paper. Then invite children to match the real shells with the shell outlines on the seashell mat.

Gone Fishing

Props: small plastic wading pool, fishing rods, assortment of plastic fish, fishing net, rubber boots, and buckets

Tie a length of string to one end of a dowel or stick to make a fishing rod. Tie a magnet to the loose end of the string. Make an assortment of plastic fish by cutting shapes from plastic coffee can lids. Attach a large paper clip to the mouth of each fish. Encourage children to pretend they are going on a fishing trip as they use the props in dramatic-play.

 School of Fish

Props: water table, plastic aquarium plants, plastic fish, small aquarium nets, small plastic tubs, pebbles or sand, and wind-up tub toys

Add plastic aquarium plants, an assortment of plastic fish, pebbles or sand, and wind-up tub toys to the water table. Invite children to use small aquarium nets to scoop up sea life. Give each child a small plastic tub to hold his or her catch.

Let's Cook

Fish Food Gorp

- round cereal
- fish-shaped crackers
- raisins
- spoons
- small baggies

Provide a large bowl of cereal, fish-shaped crackers, and raisins. Help children place spoonfuls of their favorite snacks in baggies and mix. Children can pretend to be fish as they enjoy their gorp.

Circle Time Themes

Amazing Animals

Large animals fascinate young children. The following themes combine fact and fantasy to provide extended experiences with animals.

Terrific Turkeys

Let's Look

Show a picture of a real turkey or, if possible, bring in a live turkey or visit a farm or zoo. Point out the turkey's clawlike feet, feathers, and waddle.

Let's Talk

- What is a turkey?

- What sound does a turkey make?

- What time of year do you especially think about turkeys?

- Have you ever eaten turkey?

- Where do you think turkeys live?

- What kind of house would a turkey live in?

Let's Read

Gobble, Growl, Grunt by Peter Spier

The Little Red Hen by Paul Galdone

Old MacDonald Had a Farm by Pam Aden

One Tough Turkey by Steven Kroll

Turkey on the Loose! by Sylvie Wickstrom

Wake Up, Farm by Alvin Tresselt

Who Took the Farmer's Hat? by Joan L. Nodset

Old MacDonald

Old MacDonald had a farm.
E-I-E-I-O.
And on his farm he had a cow.
E-I-E-I-O.
With a moo-moo here
and a moo-moo there.
Here a moo, there a moo,
everywhere a moo-moo.
Old MacDonald had a farm.
E-I-E-I-O.

Old MacDonald had a farm.
E-I-E-I-O.
And on his farm he had a duck.
E-I-E-I-O.
With a quack-quack here
and a quack-quack there.
Here a quack, there a quack,
everywhere a quack-quack.
A moo-moo here and
a moo-moo there,
Here a moo, there a moo,
everywhere a moo-moo.
Old MacDonald had a farm.
E-I-E-I-O.
*(Repeat with pig—oink,
horse—heeeee, chicken—cluck,
turkey—gobble, gobble, and other
favorite animals.)*

Let's Sing and Say

The Turkey

The turkey is a funny bird.
Her head goes wobble, wobble.
All she says is just one word,
"Gobble, gobble, gobble!"

Three Fat Turkeys

Three fat turkeys are we,
(Hold up three fingers.)
Hiding behind a tree.
When the cook comes around,
We don't make a sound,
For dinner we don't want to be.

Let's Move

• **Turkey Strut**

Invite children to strut like turkeys and say "Gobble, gobble, gobble." Invite children to "freeze" when you say "Gobble, gobble, gobble."

• **Turkey in the Straw**

Play a recording of the favorite old song "Turkey in the Straw." Encourage children to dance freely to the music.

Let's Make

• Turkey Feather Prints

- feathers
- tempera paint
- black construction paper

Give each child a large feather and invite children to dip the feathers in tempera paint. Then encourage children to use the feathers like paintbrushes to make designs on black construction paper.

• Turkey Balls

- clay
- feathers, pinecones, leaves, and sticks

Give each child a ball of clay (see recipe for clay #1 on page 268). Invite children to stick feathers, pinecones, leaves, and sticks into the clay to make turkeys. Be sure to accept each child's interpretation of what a turkey might look like.

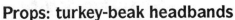

Let's Play

• Turkey Headbands

Props: turkey-beak headbands

To make the turkey-beak headbands, cut construction-paper strips long enough to fit around each child's head. Glue Velcro tabs to the ends of the strips so the headbands can be adjusted to fit snugly around children's heads. Staple construction-paper beaks to the front of the headbands. Invite children to wear the headbands as they strut and gobble like turkeys.

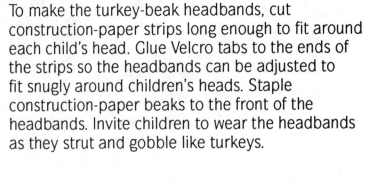

Feather Fun

Props: feathers

Provide a variety of feathers for children to sort by color, size, and shape.

Feather Dusters

Props: feather dusters

Place feather dusters in the housekeeping center. Invite children to use the feather dusters to dust the furniture in the center, as well as other areas of the classroom.

Turkey Farm

Props: boxes, sticks, toy trucks, toy turkeys, pictures of turkeys, books about turkeys, construction paper, scissors, and glue

Put small wooden or rubber turkeys and other farm animals in the block center. Discuss with children what would be needed to make a turkey farm. Invite children to make plans to build a barn and fences from blocks. Ask children to think about what they will feed the turkeys on their farm. Give children the opportunity to create a turkey farm by constructing buildings, making signs, and so on.

Let's Cook

Turkey Salad

- cooked turkey (cubed)
- pineapple chunks
- broccoli flowerets
- cheese (cubed)
- lettuce
- Ranch salad dressing
- large bowls
- small bowls (1 for each child)
- forks

Place turkey cubes, pineapple chunks, broccoli, and cheese cubes each in a separate bowl. Give each child a small bowl with 2 or 3 lettuce leaves placed on the bottom and around the sides. Invite children to make their own turkey salads, combining the turkey, fruit, cheese, and vegetables. Then pour a small amount of Ranch salad dressing on each child's salad and enjoy!

Bashful Bears

Let's Look

Bring a toy bear to circle time. Display pictures of real bears and make-believe bears as well. Invite children to bring their teddy bears from home. Encourage children to compare the bears by noticing their color, size, and other characteristics.

Let's Talk

- Do you have a teddy bear?

- What is your bear's name?

- Where did you get your bear?

- What covers a bear's body?

- Can bears talk?

- What sounds do bears make?

- What do bears like to eat?

Let's Read

Alphabears by Kathleen Hague

Ask Mr. Bear by Marjorie Flack

Bear Shadow by Frank Asch

Bears in Pairs by Niki Yektai

Berlioz the Bear by Jan Brett

Brown Bear, Brown Bear, What Do You See? by Bill Martin, Jr.

Corduroy by Don Freeman

My Brown Bear Barney by Dorothy Butler

A Pocket for Corduroy by Don Freeman

First Time Circle Time

Teddy Bear

Teddy Bear, Teddy Bear,
Turn around.
Teddy Bear, Teddy Bear,
Touch the ground.
Teddy Bear, Teddy Bear,
Go upstairs.
Teddy Bear, Teddy Bear,
Say your prayers.
Teddy Bear, Teddy Bear,
Turn out the light.
Spell goodnight.
G-O-O-D-N-I-G-H-T
Goodnight!
(Imitate designated movements.)

Polar Bear, Polar Bear, What Do You Hear? by Bill Martin, Jr.

Sleepy Bear by Lydia Dabcovich

We're Going on a Bear Hunt by Michael Rosen

Let's Sing and Say

Bears

(Tune: "Mary Had a Little Lamb")
Grizzly bears are big and brown,
Big and brown, big and brown.
Grizzly bears are big and brown,
And live in the woods.

Polar bears are soft and white,
Soft and white, soft and white.
Polar bears are soft and white,
And live where it is cold.

Teddy bears are just my size,
Just my size, just my size.
Teddy bears are just my size,
To cuddle up with at night.

Fuzzy Wuzzy

Fuzzy Wuzzy was a bear.
Fuzzy Wuzzy had no hair.
Then Fuzzy Wuzzy wasn't fuzzy, was he?

The Bear Went Over the Mountain

The bear went over the mountain,
The bear went over the mountain,
The bear went over the mountain
To see what he could see.
But all that he could see,
But all that he could see
Was the other side of the mountain,
The other side of the mountain,
The other side of the mountain
Was all that he could see.

Let's Move

- **Bear Walk**

  Encourage children to pretend they are bears by walking slowly while holding their ankles.

- **Teddy Bear Parade**

  Invite children to bring their toy and stuffed bears from home and have a teddy bear parade! Encourage children to march around the room while carrying their fuzzy friends. Play a variety of music while students march in their teddy bear parade.

Let's Make

Bear Paintings

- tempera paint (white, brown, gray, black)
- dryer lint, coffee grounds, and cotton balls
- drawing paper
- paintbrushes

Encourage children to paint bears or other simple designs at easels or at their work tables. Invite children to add dryer lint, coffee grounds, and cotton balls to the wet paint on their paper to make soft bear textures.

Fuzzy Bear Caves

- clay
- furry craft balls (pom-poms)

Invite children to make bear caves using clay (see recipe for clay #2 on page 268). Give each child a small, furry craft ball to put in their caves to represent sleeping bears.

Let's Play

Teddy Bear's Picnic

Props: picnic basket, tablecloth, tea set, and teddy bears

Place the suggested props in the housekeeping center. Or, spread the tablecloth in a carpeted area. Then invite children to have a teddy bear picnic.

Making a Picnic

Props: tablecloth or large blanket, honey sandwiches, paper bags, "beary" juice, and cups

Make honey sandwiches with the children and then invite each child to pack a honey sandwich in a paper bag. Encourage children to bring the teddy bears they have brought from home along as you go outside for a picnic. Serve "beary" juice and enjoy!

Bear Caves

Props: wet sand, small bear figures, plastic bowls, twigs, and plastic spoons

Encourage children to mold "bear caves" with wet sand. Children can use plastic bowls to mold mountains, use spoons to scoop out caves, and add twigs to represent trees. Invite children to place small bear figures in their caves.

Bear's Den

Props: blanket or sheet and bear headbands

Cover a table with a blanket or sheet. Make bear headbands from brown paper bags. Cut a strip long enough to go around each child's head and attach construction-paper ears. Encourage children to pretend that they are bears and the covered table is a bear cave.

Teddy Bear's Boutique

Props: baby or doll clothes and shoes, hair bows, small hats, small pocketbooks, headbands, full-length mirror, "open" and "closed" signs, toy cash register, bags, boxes, and price tags

Set up a teddy bear's boutique. Ask children what props should be included and ask them to help gather the materials. Make a dressing room from a large cardboard box. Attach a curtain across the front. Encourage children to make price tags and signs. Invite children to bring their teddy bears from home and "shop" for them in the boutique. Children can restock the shelves at the end of the day.

The Three Bears

Props: three chairs, three bowls, three beds (towels) in graduated sizes (small, medium, large), pots, porridge, and spoons

Tell or read the story of "The Three Bears" to the children. Invite children to suggest ways the housekeeping center could be transformed into the three bears' house using the props suggested. Then encourage children to act out the story.

Let's Cook

Three Bears' Porridge

- instant oatmeal (1 package per child)
- sunflower seeds
- raisins
- cinnamon
- honey
- spoons
- small bowls

Give each child a small bowl and an individual-size envelope of instant oatmeal. Invite the children to pour the instant oatmeal in their bowls. Add warm water to each bowl to make porridge. Provide small bowls of sunflower seeds, raisins, cinnamon, and honey for children to add to their porridge. Then enjoy the porridge with the children.

Enormous Elephants

Let's Look

Tape large, gray elephant footprints from the classroom doorway to the circle time area, ending at a closed wicker basket. Encourage children to follow the footprints to circle time. When everyone is seated, invite children to guess what is in the basket. Open the basket and take out a toy or puppet elephant. Use the elephant puppet or toy to start a discussion about elephants.

Let's Talk

- How big is an elephant?
- What do elephants look like?
- Why do elephants have big feet?
- Why do elephants have long trunks?
- What do an elephant's ears look like?
- Where do elephants live?
- Have you ever seen a live elephant? Where?

Let's Read

The Circus by Brian Wildsmith

The Circus Baby by Maud and Miska Petersham

The Elephant by Nadine Saunier

Elephant in the Jungle by Michelle Cartlidge

Five Minutes Peace by Jill Murphy

If I Were a Penguin by Heidi Goennel

The Right Number of Elephants by Jeff Sheppard

Stand Back, Said the Elephant, I'm Going to Sneeze! by Patricia Thomas

The Trouble with Elephants by Chris Riddell

Let's Sing and Say

Five Big Elephants

Five big elephants, oh, what a sight!
(Hold up five fingers.)
Swinging their trunks from left to right.
(Clasp hands in front and swing arms back and forth.)
Four are followers, and one is the king.
(Hold up four fingers, then thumb.)
They all walk around in the circus ring!
(Clasp hands in front, swing arms, and lumber like an elephant.)

I Am an Elephant

I am an elephant so big and strong,
(Stand hunched over, arms down, hands clasped in front.)
I swing my trunk as I walk along.
(Swing arms back and forth, with hands clasped in front.)
I can walk fast,
(Walk fast.)
I can walk slow,
(Lumber back and forth.)
And I can stand on one foot just so.
(Stand on one foot.)

One Little Elephant

One little elephant went out to play.
Out on a spider's web one day.
He had such enormous fun
That he called for another
little elephant to come.
(Continue to the desired number.)

Way Down South

Way down south where bananas grow,
A grasshopper stepped on an elephant's toe.
The elephant said, with tears in his eyes,
"Pick on somebody your own size."

Let's Move

Elephant Imitations

Encourage children to walk like elephants—hands together, arms straight like a trunk, and lumbering back and forth. Children can also place one foot on a large wooden block and balance like an elephant might do in a circus. Invite children to stamp and move like running elephants.

Let's Make

Elephant Trunks

- cardboard tubes (assorted sizes)

- tempera paint in shallow pans (gray and brown)

- sponges

- clothespins

- hole punch

- elastic cords

Invite each child to choose a cardboard tube and paint it shades of gray and brown using a sponge. (Attach each sponge to a clothespin to make it easier to handle.) When the paint is dry, punch holes on each side of the tube openings and tie an elastic cord through the holes. The elastic cord will hold the nose in place on the child's face.

Elephant Trunk Painting

- powdered tempera paint

- drawing paper

- spray bottles

- water

Sprinkle several colors of powdered tempera paint onto large sheets of white paper. Give children spray bottles and invite them to "spray water like an elephant" onto the paper.

Let's Play

Circus Elephants

Props: elephant ears, elephant trunks, masking tape, and hollow blocks or strong plastic crates

Collect and make an assortment of elephant props for children to use in dramatic-play. Make elephant ears from paper plates. Make trunks from cardboard tubes. Place a masking tape circle on the floor for a circus ring. Place several large hollow blocks or strong plastic crates nearby for children to use as part of the elephant act.

Blowing Elephants

Props: water table and basters

Invite children to experiment with sucking water in and squirting it out of basters, just as elephants use their trunks.

Safari

Props: jackets, hats, old cameras, and pictures of wild animals

Display pictures of wild animals around the room. Invite children to go on a photo safari using the suggested props. Children can pretend to be looking for animals to photograph as they venture on their journey.

Let's Cook

Elephant Ears

- breadstick dough
- cinnamon and sugar

Invite children to roll breadstick dough into long "snakes." Have each child wrap the bread snake around in a circular pattern to form an elephant's ear. Invite children to sprinkle cinnamon and sugar on the bread dough ears. Bake according to the package directions.

Mimicking Monkeys

Let's Look

Display a soft toy monkey in your circle time area, or hide the monkey under something. When children come to circle time, invite them to help you find the lost monkey. After he is found, discuss monkey behaviors.

Let's Talk

- Where do monkeys live?

- What do monkeys eat?

- What sounds do monkeys make?

- How do monkeys use their tails?

- How do monkeys use their hands?

Let's Read

Caps for Sale by Esphyr Slobodkina

Curious George by H.A. Rey

Curious George Goes to the Circus by Margaret Rey

Five Little Monkeys Jumping on the Bed by Eileen Christelow

Five Little Monkeys Sitting in a Tree by Eileen Christelow

I Like Books by Anthony Browne

Little Gorilla by Ruth Bornstein

Pippi Gets Lost by Helen Oxenbury

Willy the Wimp by Anthony Browne

The Animal Fair

I went to the animal fair.
The animals all were there.
The old baboon
by the light of the moon,
Was combing his auburn hair.
The monkey sure was spunk.
He climbed up
the elephant's trunk.
The elephant sneezed
and fell to his knees,
And that was the end of the
monk, monk, monk!

Five Little Monkeys Jumping on the Bed

Five little monkeys jumping on the bed.
One fell off and bumped his head.
His mother called the doctor,
and the doctor said,
"No more monkeys jumping on the bed!"

Four little monkeys jumping on the bed.
One fell off and bumped her head.
Her mother called the doctor,
and the doctor said,
"No more monkeys jumping on the bed!"

Three little monkeys jumping on the bed.
One fell off and bumped his head.
His mother called the doctor,
and the doctor said,
"No more monkeys jumping on the bed!"

Two little monkeys jumping on the bed.
One fell off and bumped her head.
Her mother called the doctor,
and the doctor said,
"No more monkeys jumping on the bed!"

One little monkey jumping on the bed.
He fell off and bumped his head.
Then there were no more monkeys
jumping on the bed!

Five Little Monkeys Swinging in a Tree

Five little monkeys swinging in a tree,
Teasing Mr. Alligator, "Can't catch me."
Along comes Mr. Alligator, happy as can be
And SNAP! Four monkeys!

Four little monkeys swinging in a tree,
Teasing Mr. Alligator, "Can't catch me."
Along comes Mr. Alligator, happy as can be
And SNAP! Three monkeys!

Three little monkeys swinging in a tree,
Teasing Mr. Alligator, "Can't catch me."
Along comes Mr. Alligator, happy as can be
And SNAP! Two monkeys!

Two little monkeys swinging in a tree,
Teasing Mr. Alligator, "Can't catch me."
Along comes Mr. Alligator, happy as can be
And SNAP! One monkey!

One little monkey swinging in a tree,
Teasing Mr. Alligator, "Can't catch me."
Along comes Mr. Alligator, happy as can be
And SNAP! No more monkeys!

(Hold up and swing five fingers. Make alligator
mouth with other hand to "snap" up the monkeys.)

Pop Goes the Weasel

All around the cobbler's bench,
The monkey chased the weasel.
The monkey thought 'twas all in fun.
Pop goes the weasel.
(Clap hands on the word "pop.")

Let's Move

Monkey in the Chair

Invite one child to sit in a chair while other children walk around him or her in a circle. The children walking in the circle sing the following song. The child in the chair stands up at the cue "so rise up on your feet" and points to another child who then becomes "it."

Here sits a monkey in the chair, chair, chair,
He (She) lost all the true loves he (she) had last year.
So rise up on your feet and greet the first you meet.
The happiest one I know.

Let's Make

Monkey Tail Painting

- brown yarn

- yellow butcher paper

- tempera paint (blue, red, green)

Braid three strands of thick brown yarn together to make 6" monkey tails. Place a monkey tail in each bowl of paint. Cover a table with yellow butcher paper. Invite children to use the yarn tails to paint on the yellow paper. Encourage children to continue until the paper is covered with colorful designs.

Monkey Playgrounds

- popsicle sticks

- cardboard tubes

- string

- glue

- wood scraps

- cardboard

Invite children to make monkey playground sculptures. Give each child a piece of cardboard as the base for the sculpture. Discuss possible monkey designs with the children before they start building.

Let's Play

Caps for Sale

Props: baseball caps, sporting caps, caps worn by food workers, caps worn by military personnel, sailor's caps, berets, painter's caps, mirror, and cash register

Invite children to help you set up a "Peddler's Cap Shop." Collect and arrange a variety of caps. Encourage children to role-play buying, selling, and wearing caps. Read *Caps for Sale* to the children, if you wish.

Monkey Bars

Props: indoor climber, monkey headbands, and cardboard trees

Set up an indoor climber and tape cardboard trees to each side. Provide monkey headbands made from construction paper with monkey ears taped to the bands. Encourage children to pretend to be monkeys climbing in the trees.

Let's Cook

Monkey Munchies

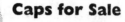

- bananas
- plastic knives
- peanut butter

Give each child a banana. Help children peel their bananas. Then cut each child's banana in half lengthwise. Invite the children to spread the bananas with peanut butter and then enjoy the tasty snack.

Circle Time Themes

Marvelous Munchies

Preparing healthy snacks provides extended experiences with mixing and pouring. The cooking themes in this section provide opportunities for children to sample new foods, observe the effects of temperature on food, and use simple kitchen tools.

Pizza Pizzaz

Let's Look

Bring a basket of supplies that could be used to make a pizza to circle time. Encourage children to guess what you will make with the supplies. Look at each item and point out its size, shape, color, taste, and purpose.

Let's Talk

- What is a pizza?

- Do you like to eat pizza?

- Is pizza good for you?

- What shape is a pizza?

- How do you make a pizza?

- What foods make you healthy?

- What happens if you only eat junk food?

Let's Read

Bread, Bread, Bread by Ann Morris

Curious George and the Pizza by Margaret Rey

Daddy Makes the Best Spaghetti by Anna Grossnickle Hines

The Lady with the Alligator Purse by Nadine B. Westcott

Little Nino's Pizzeria by Karen Barbour

Pizza Man by Marjorie Pillar

Let's Sing and Say

I Like Pizza

(Tune: "La Cucaracha")
I like a pizza,
I like a pizza,
La-la-la-la-la-la-la.
(Repeat)

Additional Verses:
I make a pizza...
I slice a pizza...
I eat a pizza...
(Imitate movements.)

My Father Owns the Butcher Shop

My father owns the butcher shop.
My mother cuts the meat.
And I'm the little hot dog
That runs around the street.

Simple Simon

Simple Simon met a pieman
going to the fair.
Said Simple Simon to the pieman,
"Let me taste your ware."
Said the pieman to Simple Simon,
"Show me first your penny."
Said Simple Simon to the pieman,
"Indeed, I have not any."

Here Are My Lady's Knives and Forks

Here are my lady's knives and forks.
(Interlock fingers to indicate knives and forks.)
Here is father's table.
(Keeping fingers interlocked, turn hands over
so fingers form tabletop and wrists form legs.)
Here is sister's looking glass.
(Raise one hand to eye, fingers forming circle.)
And here is baby's cradle.
(Rock hands like a cradle.)

Pat-a-Cake

Pat-a-cake, pat-a-cake, baker's man.
(Clap hands.)
Bake me a cake just as fast as you can.
(Clap hands.)
Pat it and shape it and mark it with a B,
(Pat, mold, and mark hand with other hand.)
And put it in the oven for baby and me.
(Imitate putting cake in the oven,
then point away and to self.)

Let's Move

Pizza Circle Dance

Give each child a cardboard pizza circle. Encourage
children to discuss all the ways they could move
with and around the circle. Children might suggest
walking around the circle, standing on top of the
circle, standing under the circle, or jumping over the
circle. Play a dance record and invite children to
move around their pizza circles.

Let's Make

Pizza Rounds

- clay (see recipe for clay #2 on page 268)
- empty spools
- straws
- tempera paint or watercolors
- non-toxic liquid polymer or white glue

Give each child a ball of clay. Invite children to make pizzas by flattening the clay. Children can make prints on the "pizza dough" using empty spools, straw, or other tools. Invite children to paint the dried clay pizzas using tempera paint or watercolors. When the paint is dry, seal the finished pizzas by coating them with non-toxic liquid polymer or watered-down white glue.

Pizza Playdough

- empty water table or large tub
- flour
- salt
- small plastic bowls
- water pitchers

Invite children to experiment mixing flour, salt, and water in their own individual bowls to make playdough. Have children do the mixing over an empty water table or large tub to catch any spills. This activity needs careful supervision and is best done after children have had an opportunity to make playdough with teacher guidance.

Let's Play

Pizza Parlor

Props: round pizza pans, spatulas, cardboard pizzas, chef hats, aprons, potholders, pads and pencils, table, chairs, cash register, play money, and menus

Set up a pizza parlor in your classroom or learning center. Invite children to pretend to be customers and employees at a pizza restaurant using the suggested props.

Let's Cook

Pita Pizza

- plastic knives
- spoon

- pita bread
- tomato sauce
- mozzarella cheese

Cut the pita bread pockets in half and give each child a round pita circle. Place a spoonful of tomato sauce in the center of each circle. Invite children to spread the tomato sauce on their pita circles and then place a slice of cheese on top. Place the pita pizzas on cookie sheets and bake at 350° F until the cheese melts.

Scrumptious Soup

Let's Look

Prepare a mystery bag for each child by placing fresh vegetables in several different paper bags. Use an assortment of vegetables, such as green beans, new potatoes, peppers, crook-neck squash, and so on. Invite children to discuss what might be in their bags. After the children have made a guess, invite children to open their bags and find out if their guesses were correct. Then place all the vegetables in a colander and save them to make vegetable soup.

Let's Talk

- What is in your bag?

- What can we do with these vegetables?

- What is soup?

- How many kinds of soup can you name?

- Do you usually eat soup when it is hot or cold?

- What is a recipe?

- What is your favorite recipe?

Let's Read

Eating the Alphabet: Fruits and Vegetables from A to Z by Lois Ehlert

The Giant Vegetable Garden by Nadine B. Westcott

Growing Vegetable Soup by Lois Ehlert

Soup for Supper by Phyllis Root

Stone Soup by Ann McGovern

We Keep a Store by Anne Shelby

Let's Sing and Say

Old MacDonald's Veggie Patch

(Tune: "Old MacDonald Had a Farm")
Old MacDonald had a farm. E-I-E-I-O.
And on his farm he grew some carrots.
E-I-E-I-O.
With a crunch, crunch here
and a crunch, crunch there
Here a crunch, there a crunch,
everywhere a crunch, crunch.
Old MacDonald had a farm. E-I-E-I-O.

Old MacDonald had a farm. E-I-E-I-O.
And on his farm he grew potatoes.
E-I-E-I-O.
With a mash, mash here
and a mash, mash there
Here a mash, there a mash,
everywhere a mash, mash.
Old MacDonald had a farm. E-I-E-I-O.

Old MacDonald had a farm. E-I-E-I-O.
And on his farm he grew some lettuce.
E-I-E-I-O.
With a toss, toss here
and a toss, toss there
Here a toss, there a toss,
everywhere a toss, toss.
Old MacDonald had a farm. E-I-E-I-O.

Polly Put the Kettle On

Polly put the kettle on, Polly put the kettle on,
Polly put the kettle on, we'll all have soup.
Sukey take it off again, Sukey take it off again,
Sukey take it off again, they've all gone home.

The Soup Is Boiling Hot

(Tune: "Farmer in the Dell")
The soup is boiling hot.
The soup is boiling hot.
Stir, pour, we'll eat some more.
The soup is boiling hot.

First we'll add some broth.
First we'll add some broth.
Stir, pour, we'll eat some more.
First we'll add some broth.

Next we'll add some beans.
Next we'll add some beans.
Stir, pour, we'll eat some more.
Next we'll add some beans.
(Continue verses adding ingredients.)

Oats, Peas, Beans

Oats, peas, beans, and barley grow.
Oats, peas, beans, and barley grow.
Do you or I or anyone know
How oats, peas, beans, and barley grow?
(Join hands with the children and skip around in a circle.)

First the farmer sows her seeds.
Then she stands and takes her ease,
Stamps her feet, and claps her hand;
And turns around to view her land.
(One child role-plays the farmer, stands in the middle, and acts out the words.)

Pease Porridge Hot

Pease porridge hot, pease porridge cold,
Pease porridge in the pot nine days old.
Some like it hot, and some like it cold.
I like it in the pot nine days old!

Let's Move

• Vegetable Soup Scramble

Invite children to hold hands and move in a circle while music is playing. After a brief period, stop the music and say "Vegetable soup scramble." Children all run to the center of the circle and dance around. When the music resumes, children return to the circle perimeter and the game continues.

Let's Make

• Vegetable Prints

- liquid starch

- powdered tempera paint (red, green, orange, yellow)

- sponges

- shallow aluminum pans

- drawing paper

- vegetable pieces (potatoes, carrots, celery)

- knife (for teacher use only)

Mix liquid starch with powdered tempera and water to form a thick paint. Place a thin sponge in the bottom of each shallow aluminum pan. Spread the paint mixture over each sponge. Then cut the vegetables to make stamps for printing. Invite children to make prints by pressing a vegetable on a print pad (sponge) and then onto paper. Use carrot tops and other vegetable "scraps" to avoid wasting food.

Vegetable Baskets

- clay (see recipe for clay #1 on page 268)
- tempera paint
- paintbrushes
- strawberry baskets or styrofoam meat trays

Encourage children to make vegetable shapes out of clay. Allow the clay vegetables to dry and then invite children to paint them. Display the finished vegetables in strawberry baskets or on styrofoam meat trays.

Let's Play

The Green Grocer's Store

Props: empty food boxes and cans, grocer's aprons, paper or cloth bags, vegetable scale, cash register, child-sized grocery carts, boxes, feather duster, tagboard, and crayons or markers

Set up a grocery store in your classroom. Recycle empty food boxes and cans for your grocery stock. Encourage children to purchase and bag groceries, restock and dust shelves, and make shelf-marker signs.

Let's Cook

Scrumptious Vegetable Soup

- vegetables
- vegetable brushes and peeler
- knife (for teacher use only)
- salt and pepper

- chicken broth (6 oz can for every 4 children)
- large pot
- ladle
- spoons

Use the vegetables from the mystery bags plus vegetables brought from home by you and the children for the soup. Invite children to help wash the vegetables. Peel and chop the vegetables and set aside. Put the chicken broth in a large pot and heat. Add the vegetables and cook until the vegetables are tender.

Perfect Peanut Butter

Let's Look

Pass around a bowl of peanuts in the shell. Invite children to pick up the peanuts and shake them. Encourage children to guess what is inside the shells. Then pass around a jar of peanut butter. Ask the children if they know what peanut butter is made of.

Let's Talk

- What is peanut butter?

- How is it made?

- Do you like to eat peanut butter?

- What animals like peanuts?

- Is peanut butter good for you?

- How does peanut butter taste?

- Why do you think peanuts have shells?

- What do you eat peanut butter with?

Let's Read

Eat up, Gemma by Sarah Hayes

From Grain to Bread by Ali Mitgutsch

The Giant Jam Sandwich by John Vernon Lord and Janet Burroway

In Between by Monica Wellington

Jamberry by Bruce Degen

Peanut Butter and Jelly: A Play Rhyme by Nadine B. Westcott

Let's Sing and Say

Peanut Butter

Peanut, peanut butter,
(Whisper "Jelly.")
Peanut, peanut butter,
(Whisper "Jelly.")
First you take the peanuts
and you smash 'em, you smash 'em,
You smash 'em, smash 'em, smash 'em.
(Imitate smashing peanuts.)
Then you take the peanut butter
and you spread it, you spread it,
You spread it, spread it, spread it.
(Imitate spreading peanut butter.)

Peanut, peanut butter,
(Whisper "Jelly.")
Peanut, peanut butter,
(Whisper "Jelly.")
Then you take the grapes
and you squish 'em, you squish 'em,
You squish 'em, squish 'em, squish 'em.
(Imitate squishing.)
And then you take the jelly
and you spread it, you spread it,
You spread it, spread it, spread it.
(Imitate spreading.)
Peanut, peanut butter,
(Whisper "Jelly.")
Peanut, peanut butter,
(Whisper "Jelly.")
Then you put the bread together
and you cut it, you cut it.
You cut it, cut it, cut it.
(Imitate cutting.)
Then you munch it, you munch it,
You munch it, munch it, munch it.
(Imitate chewing and swallowing.)
Peanut, peanut butter,
(Whisper "Jelly.")
Peanut, peanut butter,
(Whisper "Jelly.")

Toot! Toot!

A peanut sat on a railroad track;
His heart was all aflutter.
The five-fifteen came rushing by—
Toot! Toot! Peanut butter!

Jelly

Jelly on my head,
Jelly on my toes,
Jelly on my coat,
Jelly on my nose.
Laughing and a-licking.
Having me a time,
Jelly on my belly,
But I like it fine.

Jelly is my favorite food,
And when I'm in a jelly mood,
I can't ever get enough
Of that yummy, gummy stuff.

Pretty soon it will be spring,
And I'll do my gardening,
But I'll plant no flowerbed;
I'll plant jelly beans instead.

I'm a Nut

I'm a nut, small and round,
Lying on the cold, cold ground.
People pass and step on me.
That's why I'm all cracked, you see.
I'm a nut *(clap, clap)*.
I'm a nut *(clap, clap)*.
I'm a nut *(clap, clap)*.
I'm a nut *(clap, clap)*.

Let's Move

• Peanut Balance

Invite children to balance a peanut on their shoulders or on spoons while they walk around the classroom or playground. Just for fun, invite children to try holding a peanut between their nose and upper lip or balance the peanut on their heads.

Let's Make

• Peanut-Shell Collages

- cardboard

- scissors

- collage materials, such as peanut shells, paper scraps, wood shavings, and straw

- glue

Cut cardboard into a variety of sizes and shapes. Give each child a piece and then invite children to glue collage materials to the cardboard to make interesting designs.

• Peanut-Butter Bird Treats

- toasted bread (one slice per child)

- cookie cutters

- creamy peanut butter

- bird seed

- chenille pipe cleaners

- plastic knives

Give each child a slice of toasted bread. Invite children to use cookie cutters to cut shapes from the bread. Have children spread one side of the bread shapes with creamy peanut butter and then sprinkle with bird seed. Push a chenille stem through each slice of bread and twist the top to make a hanger. Hang the bird treats from a nearby tree branch for the children to observe.

Let's Play

Peanut Farmers

Props: peanuts in the shell, peat pots, and potting soil

Soak peanuts (in the shell) in water overnight. Provide a gardener's peat pot for each child and enough potting soil to fill it. Give each child a soaked peanut to plant in his or her pot. Place the pots in a sunny window and help the children water their pots regularly. Watch for sprouts.

Digging for Peanuts

Props: sand table, peanuts, spoons, tongs, and small scoops

To remind children that peanuts grow underground, bury shelled peanuts in the sand table for children to find. When all the peanuts have been "harvested," bury them again for a game of digging for peanuts at another time.

Let's Cook

Peanut Butter

- peanuts (in the shell)
- vegetable oil
- crackers
- plastic knives
- small paper plates

Invite children to shell the peanuts. Place the shelled peanuts in a blender and add 1 tablespoon of vegetable oil. Blend well. Give each child 1 tablespoon of peanut butter and several crackers on a paper plate. Invite children to spread the peanut butter on the crackers and enjoy their snack of homemade peanut butter. (Be aware of any allergies to peanuts in the classroom.)

Frozen Flavors

Let's Look

Give each child an ice cube to hold. Invite children to watch what happens to the ice as they hold it in their warm hands. Or, give each child a paper cup filled with ice. Challenge children to place their cups of ice in a spot where they think the ice won't melt. Check the cups in a short while and then again later. Discuss the results.

Let's Talk

- What is ice?

- What does ice do to food?

- What is ice cream?

- What flavors of ice cream can you name?

- How does ice cream feel?

- What happens to ice cream when it is not in the freezer?

- When do you like to eat ice cream?

- What is your favorite flavor of ice cream?

Let's Read

From Milk to Ice Cream by Ali Mitgutsch

Ice Cream by Jill Neimark

Let's Eat by Gyo Fujikawa

Spot's Birthday Party by Eric Hill

The Very Hungry Caterpillar by Eric Carle

What Was It Before It Was Ice Cream? by Colleen L. Reece

Let's Sing and Say

I Scream

I scream,
you scream
We all scream
for ice cream.

My Ice-Cream Cone

See my ice-cream cone so very tall?
(Hold hand as if holding a cone.)
See the ice cream in a ball?
*(Form fingers into a ball,
placing fist over the pretend cone.)*
When I take a big lick with my tongue,
(Pretend to lick.)
It goes down to my tummy.
Yum! Yum! Yum!
(Rub tummy.)

I Like Ice Cream

(Tune: "Frere Jacques")
I like ice cream,
I like ice cream,
On a cone,
On a cone.
Lemon and vanilla,
Chocolate and cherry,
I like them all,
I like them all.

I like ice cream,
I like ice cream,
On some pie,
On some pie.
Lemon and vanilla,
Chocolate and cherry,
It's hard to choose,
It's hard to choose.

The Ice-Cream Spot

(Tune: "Mary Had a Little Lamb")
When the sun is very hot,
very hot, very hot,
When the sun is very hot,
My mom takes me to
the ice-cream spot.

We walk together holding hands,
holding hands, holding hands.
We walk together holding hands,
On our way to the ice-cream stand.

We sit upon the shiny stool,
shiny stool, shiny stool.
We sit upon the shiny stool,
And order ice cream, nice and cool.

The Ice-Cream Shop

See the yummy ice-cream cones in a row,
(Hold up four fingers and pretend to count.)
Waiting for a little child to buy one to go.
Mary took a cherry one,
(Point to and name a child.)
Brent took one, too.
(Continue pointing.)
Patrick took a chocolate one,
And here's one for you.
(Point to the last child.)

Let's Move

- **Ice-Cream Shop**

  Invite children to pantomime going to the ice-cream shop, paying for ice cream, holding the cone, walking with the ice cream, eating the ice cream, and having sticky hands.

Let's Make

Ice Cube Painting

- dry tempera paint

- white drawing paper

- styrofoam meat trays

- ice cubes

Place white drawing paper on styrofoam trays. Give each child a tray and invite children to sprinkle several colors of dry tempera paint on the paper. Then have each child place an ice cube on one corner of his or her paper and slowly tilt the tray. The ice cubes will mix the paint as they move across the paper, making colorful designs.

Build an Ice-Cream Cone

- construction paper
- scissors
- glue
- corrugated cardboard
- cotton balls (assorted colors)

Cut the corrugated cardboard into triangle shapes. Invite each child to choose a cardboard triangle shape to glue on a piece of construction paper as an ice-cream cone. (Older children can cut their own triangle cone shapes.) Encourage children to glue cotton balls on top of their cones to represent scoops of ice cream.

Let's Play

Ice-Cream Parlor

Props: table, chairs, cups, spoons, and menus

Set up an ice-cream parlor in your classroom. Invite children to suggest prop ideas. Encourage children to use the props to role-play being customers and parlor managers in the classroom ice-cream parlor.

Frozen Sculptures

Props: water table and plastic containers

Fill various sizes of large plastic containers with water and freeze them to make ice blocks. Place the ice blocks in the water table. Invite children to stack the blocks to form sculptures.

Let's Cook

Icees

• 6 oz frozen fruit juice
• 1 pint yogurt

• paper cups (3 oz size)
• popsicle sticks (one per child)

Combine the fruit juice and yogurt in a blender. Pour the mixture into small paper cups. Insert a popsicle stick into each cup and then freeze. When frozen, invite children to peel away the paper cups and enjoy their frozen treats.

Circle Time Themes

Family Feasts and Festivals

In this section, young children are given the opportunity to learn to give to others. The themes featured introduce children to special "giving times" and provide activities that include gift making, cooking, and making developmentally appropriate crafts.

Fabulous Feasts

Let's Look

Fill a small wagon with "harvest foods," such as pumpkins, acorn squash, and potatoes. Park the wagon near the circle area. Invite one child to pull the wagon to circle time. Encourage children to observe the colors, shapes, and sizes of the vegetables. (If a wagon is not available, use a large basket.)

Let's Talk

- When do you eat foods like the ones in the wagon?

- Do you ever have special dinners at your home?

- Have you ever gone to a relative's home for a special dinner?

- What do you eat at special dinners?

- Who cooks the food for special dinners?

- Do you help cook, set the table, or clean your home?

- What are some ways you could decorate a dinner table?

- At what times of the year do you have special family feasts?

Let's Read

Apples and Pumpkins by Anne Rockwell

At Grammy's House by Eve Rice

How Many Days to America? by Eve Bunting

Nice and Clean by Anne and Harlow Rockwell

Over the River and Through the Wood by Lydia Maria Child

Pumpkin Pumpkin by Jeanne Titherington

Thanksgiving Treat by Catherine Stock

First Time Circle Time

Let's Sing and Say

Here We Are Together

(Tune: "The More We Get Together")
Here we are together, together, together.
Here we are together sharing a meal.
There's Grandma and Grandpa
and Mother and Dad.
Here we are together sharing a meal.

(Be sensitive to the variety of family structures
among your students. Discuss family members
and adapt the song to meet your students' needs.)

The Feast

Here we are together
sitting at the table.
(Hold up fingers of one hand.)
Here is Mother.
(Point to thumb.)
Here is my step-dad.
(Point to pointer.)
Here is Grandpa.
(Point to third finger.)
Here is my sister.
(Point to ring finger.)
Here I am.
(Point to little finger.)

(Be sensitive to the variety of
family structures among your
students. Discuss family
members and adapt the song
to meet your students' needs.)

Pumpkin Pie

First you cook the pumpkin
'til it's done,
(Imitate opening and closing oven door.)
Then you put it in a bowl
and mash it some.
(Imitate mashing.)
Add some spices, milk,
eggs, and honey,
(Imitate sprinkling, pouring,
and cracking eggs.)
And stir it some more
until it's yummy.
(Stir and then rub stomach.)
Pour it in a pie shell
and bake it right,
(Imitate cooking.)
Let it cook a little
for dinner tonight.
(Rub stomach again.)

The Harvest

(Tune: "The Farmer in the Dell")
The harvest time is here,
The harvest time is here,
Hi-ho and derry-o,
The harvest time is here.

The farmer picks the squash,
The farmer picks the squash,
Hi-ho and derry-o,
The farmer picks the squash.

The farmer cuts the cane,
The farmer cuts the cane,
Hi-ho and derry-o,
The farmer cuts the cane.

He (She) loads it in the truck,
He (She) loads it in the truck,
Hi-ho, the derry-o,
He (She) loads it in the truck.

We're Thankful

We're thankful for the food we eat,
We're thankful for the friends we meet,
We're thankful for the golden sun,
The trees, the birds, and everyone.

She'll Be Coming 'Round the Mountain

She'll be coming 'round the mountain when she comes. Toot, toot!
She'll be coming 'round the mountain when she comes. Toot, toot!
She'll be coming 'round the mountain, she'll be coming 'round the mountain,
She'll be coming 'round the mountain when she comes. Toot, toot!

She'll be driving six white horses when she comes. Whoa, back!
She'll be driving six white horses when she comes. Whoa, back!
She'll be driving six white horses, she'll be driving six white horses,
She'll be driving six white horses when she comes. Whoa, back!

We'll all go out to meet her when she comes. Hi, there!
We'll all go out to meet her when she comes. Hi, there!
We'll all go out to meet her, we'll all go out to meet her,
We'll all go out to meet her when she comes. Hi, there!

We'll all eat chicken and dumplings when she comes. Mmm, mmm!
We'll all eat chicken and dumplings when she comes. Mmm, mmm!
We'll all eat chicken and dumplings, we'll all eat chicken and dumplings,
We'll all eat chicken and dumplings when she comes. Mmm, mmm!

Mabel, Mabel

Mabel, Mabel, set the table,
Don't forget the salt and pepper.
(Slap thighs, clap hands,
slap partner's hands one at a time.
Repeat the rhyme faster each time.)

Let's Move

• Feast Foods

Invite children to jump like lettuce being tossed in a salad, twirl like potatoes being mashed with a mixer, shake like jiggly Jello, and hop up and down like popping popcorn. Encourage children to suggest movements for other feast foods as well.

Let's Make

• A Tablecloth

- white cotton fabric
- newspaper
- tape
- crayons
- iron (for teacher use only)

Cover a table with newspaper. Tape a piece of white fabric over the newspaper. Invite children to decorate the cloth using crayons. Cover the finished cloth with newspaper and iron each section to seal the wax crayon designs.

Placemats

- construction paper
- tissue paper
- confetti
- glue (colored)
- clear contact paper or laminating machine

Invite children to design placemat collages on sheets of construction paper. Encourage children to use tissue paper, confetti, and colored glue to decorate their collages. When the placemats are completely dry, cover each placemat with clear contact paper or laminate the mats. Encourage children to make one placemat for each family member and take the mats home to use at a special dinner.

Let's Play

Company's Coming

Props: candlestick and candles, cloth napkins, napkin rings, vase of flowers, place cards, dishes and flatware, pitcher or silver pot, empty squirt bottles, and dust cloths

Invite children to prepare an area of the classroom for guests as they set the table and clean the house. Suggest to the children that they pretend to have a meal with their special "guests."

Let's Cook

Cornbread and Butter

- cornbread mix
- muffin tins
- baby-food jars (one per child)
- cream (room temperature)
- cranberry jam
- plastic knives

Invite children to help mix the cornbread according to the package directions. Spoon the mixture into muffin tins and bake. While the cornbread is baking, give each child a baby-food jar half full of cream. Invite children to shake the jar until the cream forms a small ball of butter. (You can add a little yellow food coloring and salt, if desired.) Drain the liquid (buttermilk) from the jar. Children can then spread their homemade butter and some cranberry jam on the warm corn muffins. Invite family members to visit the classroom and share the snacks.

Love Notes

Let's Look

Bring a real or cardboard mailbox containing letters and valentines to circle time. Have the flag up indicating that there is mail inside the box. Invite children to observe the way this mailbox is made and to consider its function. After the children guess what might be inside, open the box and invite children to look at the contents. Give each child a valentine or postcard addressed especially to him or her.

Let's Talk

- Do you have a mailbox?

- What are mailboxes for?

- Who delivers letters to your home?

- What are valentines?

- Have you ever received a valentine or letter from a friend?

- Have you ever made a valentine for someone?

- What do valentines often say?

- What are some other ways you can let someone know that you love them?

Let's Read

Ask Mr. Bear by Marjorie Flack

A Book of Hugs by Dave Ross

Four Valentines in a Rainstorm by Felicia Bond

Just for You by Mercer Mayer

Love from Aunt Betty by Nancy Winslow Parker

Loving by Ann Morris

Mama, Do You Love Me? by Barbara M. Joosse

Say It by Charlotte Zolotow

The Valentine Bears by Eve Bunting

Let's Sing and Say

Roses Are Red

Roses are red.
Violets are blue.
Sugar is sweet,
And so are YOU!

Question

Do you love me,
Or do you not?
You told me once,
But I forgot.

Love Somebody, Yes, I Do

Love somebody, yes, I do,
Love somebody, yes, I do,
Love somebody, yes, I do,
Love somebody, but I won't tell who.

Love my Daddy, yes, I do,
Love my Daddy, yes, I do,
Love my Daddy, yes, I do,
Love my Daddy and he loves me, too.

Additional Verses:
Love my Mommy, yes, I do...
Love my Sister, yes, I do...
Love my Grandpa, yes, I do...
(Be sensitive to a variety of family structures and adapt accordingly.)

Let's Move

Partner Connection

Encourage children to dance together with
partners. Have each partner hold the end of a
single piece of yarn to "connect friends."
Play different styles of music to set a variety of
dancing moods.

Let's Make

Heart Pouch

- pinking shears (for teacher use only)
- burlap (red, pink, purple, or lavender)
- yarn and plastic darning needle
- scraps of paper, foil, net, doilies, and ribbon
- glue

Using pinking shears, cut burlap into 6" x 12" pieces. Fold each piece of burlap in half to form a 6" square. Cut a large heart from each folded piece of fabric to make two identical hearts connected by the fold at the bottom. Place the cut-out hearts flat on a table. Invite children to glue pieces of foil, net, doily, ribbon, yarn, and paper to the burlap hearts. When the decorations are complete, invite children to lace the sides of the hearts together leaving the top open. Stitch a ribbon across opposite sides at the top of each heart to make carry-sacks out of the heart pouches.

Valentine Shadow Boxes

- shallow boxes (one per child)
- tempera paint (pink, white, and red)
- paintbrushes
- strips of tissue paper, doilies, and ribbon
- construction-paper hearts
- liquid laundry starch or glue

Give each child a shallow box (valentine boxes are a good source). Add a small amount of liquid laundry starch or glue to tempera paint. Invite each child to paint the inside of a shallow box with tempera paint. Children can place strips of tissue paper, doilies, ribbon and construction-paper hearts on the wet paint to make collages. Encourage children to give the decorated boxes to a friend or family member.

Let's Play

Letter Writing

Props: construction paper, plain paper, stationery, unlined index cards, markers, stickers, rubber stamps, envelopes, staplers, scissors, and glue sticks

Set up a letter-writing center. Encourage children to pretend to "write" letters (don't worry about children's spelling).

Postal Carriers

Props: cardboard boxes, mailbag, and slotted box

Cut a mail slot in one side of a large cardboard box. Place a smaller box inside, beneath the slot, to catch the mail. Encourage children to use the slotted box to send mail to their friends or family members. Give children the opportunity to explore this center by mailing letters, collecting the mail in the mailbag, and delivering the letters to the mailboxes.

Let's Cook

Heart Sandwiches

- white bread (1 slice per child)
- heart-shaped cookie cutters
- cream cheese (softened)
- strawberry fruit spread (low sugar)
- plastic knives

Invite children to use cookie cutters to cut slices of bread into heart shapes. Help children spread their bread hearts with cream cheese. Encourage children to put a spoonful of fruit spread in the middle. Enjoy heart sandwiches with the children.

In Honor of Families

Let's Look

Collect pictures of families, including your own. Ask children to bring in family pictures as well as cut out family pictures from magazines. Include pictures depicting family members of all ages and different ethnic backgrounds. Also, be sure to include a variety of family structures (single parent, small and large families). Display the pictures on a low easel and cover them with a drape. Reveal and discuss each family portrait one at a time.

Let's Talk

- Who lives in your home?

- Do you have relatives who live with you?

- Who is the oldest person in your family?

- Who is the youngest person in your family?

- How do you help your family?

- How does your family work together?

- What games do you play with your family?

- Do you share special activities (TV, stories, sports) together?

Let's Read

Friday Night Is Papa Night by Ruth Sonneborn

Grandma Gets Grumpy by Anna Grossnickle Hines

Just Like Daddy by Frank Asch

Just Me and My Mom by Mercer Mayer

Mama, Do You Love Me? by Barbara M. Joosse

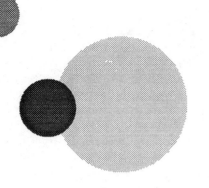

My Mom Travels a Lot by Caroline Feller Bauer

Now One Foot, Now the Other by Tomie dePaola

On Mother's Lap by Ann H. Scott

The Relatives Came by Cynthia Rylant

We Keep a Store by Anne Shelby

Let's Sing and Say

Are You Sleeping?

(Tune: "Frere Jacques")
Are you sleeping, are you sleeping?
(Children pretend to be asleep.)
Brother John, Brother John?
Morning bells are ringing.
Morning bells are ringing.
Ding, ding, dong.
(Ring a bell to awaken children.)
Ding, ding, dong.
(Substitute children's names for "Brother John.")

Fine Family

Here is the family in my household.
(Hold up five fingers.)
Some are young,
(Move thumb.)
And some are old.
(Move index finger.)
Some are tall,
(Move middle finger.)
Some are small.
(Move ring finger.)
Some are growing just like me.
(Move little finger.)
Together we all live as a family.
(Move all five fingers.)

Here Is Baby's Tossled Head

Here is baby's tossled head.
(Make a fist.)
He nods, and nods,
(Bend wrist, bobbing fist up and down.)
Let's put him to bed.
(Bend other arm and tuck fist in at elbow.)

Let's Move

 Family Members

Encourage children to take long-legged daddy steps, crawl like a baby, jog like an older brother or sister, or walk more slowly like a grandma or grandpa.

Let's Make

Treasure Boxes

- small boxes (one per child)

- beads or discarded jewelry

- collage materials, such as ribbon, rickrack, sequins, and buttons

- glitter

- glue

- tissue paper

Have each child select a small box and remove the lid. Invite children to cover the lid with white glue and select jewels, sequins, ribbon, and other collage materials to decorate the box top. Allow the lids to dry thoroughly and then place them back on the boxes. Children can then wrap the decorated treasure boxes in tissue and tie the bags with decorative ribbon. Invite children to give their treasure boxes as gifts.

Framed Stitchery

- white burlap

- scissors

- wooden craft beads

- large, plastic darning needles

- yarn (several colors)

- lace, feathers, ribbon

- glue

- cardboard

- fabric or construction paper

Cut burlap into 6" squares. Thread large plastic, darning needles with yarn. Tie a wooden bead to the free end of each piece of yarn and tie the other end securely around the needle eye to prevent it from slipping out. Show children how to make stitches on the burlap with a variety of yarn colors. Supervise children carefully to prevent them from pulling the stitches too tightly or knotting the work. Children can glue ribbon, lace, beads, and feathers on the burlap square for decoration. When completed, mount the decorated burlap squares on 8" cardboard squares that have been covered with fabric or construction paper. Glue a ribbon loop to the back so the framed stitchery pictures can be hung on a wall. Suggest that the children give their framed stitchery as gifts.

Family Books

- photographs of children and their families

- posterboard

- hole punch

- glue

- yarn

Make photocopies of the pictures that the children bring to school. Cut and mount the photocopies on posterboard pages. Punch holes in the side of each page and thread the pages together with yarn. Ask each child to dictate a sentence about his or her family to go under the picture. If the child does not have a photograph to bring, let him or her draw a picture for the class book. Place the book in the reading corner.

Let's Play

Families

Props: variety of dress-up clothes (shirts, ties, vests, shoes, dresses, hats), pocketbooks, jewelry, broken camera, electric shaver (cord removed), telephone, telephone directory, magazines, newspaper, and small suitcases

Place props in a special area in the classroom to encourage family role-playing.

Doll Families

Props: doll house and bendable family figures

Place a doll house and bendable family figures in the manipulative area. If you do not have a sturdy doll house, make separate rooms out of shoeboxes. Glue the box rooms together to make a house. Make cardboard box furniture to fill the rooms. If you do not have bendable family figures, cut family member pictures from magazines and mount them on cardboard.

Block Families

Props: rubber family figures or small dolls and blocks

Place rubber family figures or small dolls in the block center to encourage house construction and family play.

Gallery of Families

Props: bulletin board and family pictures

Prepare a bulletin board of family pictures including pictures that the children bring to school of their families. (Be sensitive to each child's family situation.)

Let's Cook

Sunshine Bagels

- mini-bagels (1/2 per child)
- margarine
- plastic knives
- cheddar cheese (grated)
- mayonnaise (low-fat)
- juice
- paper cups

Give each child a bagel half. Invite children to cover their bagels with margarine. Combine the grated cheese and enough mayonnaise to make a spread. Have children spread the mixture on their bagels. Place the bagels on a cookie sheet and heat under the broiler until the cheese is melted and begins to bubble. Cool. Serve with juice. You may want to ask the children to each invite a family member to come to class to share their snack.

Best Birthdays

Let's Look

Place birthday party items, such as balloons, party hats, blowers, candles, and wrapped presents, inside a large, brightly wrapped box. Invite children to examine the box, unwrap it, and name the items inside.

Let's Talk

- What is a birthday?

- Have you ever had a cake with candles on it? When?

- What other special foods do you eat on your birthday?

- What special things do people do on their birthdays?

- What might you wish for on your birthday?

- How old are you?

- What can you do now that you couldn't do when you were a baby?

- What will you be able to do when you are grown up that you can't do now?

Let's Read

Alfie Gives a Hand by Shirley Hughes

Alice's Blue Cloth by Deborah VanDerBeek

The Birthday Party by Helen Oxenbury

Birthday Wishes by Ann Schweninger

Happy Birthday Dear Duck by Eve Bunting

Happy Birthday, Grampie by Susan Pearson

Happy Birthday Moon by Frank Asch

Happy Birthday Sam by Pat Hutchins

Hello, Amigos! by Tricia Brown

On the Day You Were Born
by Debra Frasier

Peabody by Rosemary Wells

The Wednesday Surprise
by Eve Bunting

Four Pretty Presents

Four pretty presents
and they are all for me.
(Hold up four fingers.)
I unwrapped the red one,
and now there are three.
Three pretty presents
and one is from you.
(Hold up three fingers.)
I unwrapped the blue one,
and now there are two.
Two pretty presents
left until I'm done.
(Hold up two fingers.)
I unwrapped the yellow one
and now there is one.
One pretty present,
I am having so much fun!
(Hold up one finger.)
I unwrapped it slowly,
and now there are none.
*(Hold up both hands,
palms facing out.)*

Let's Sing and Say

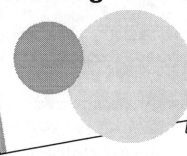

The Package

Here is the package
so brightly wrapped.
(Hold an imaginary package.)
Inside is a secret
that is well kept.
Now let's take the ribbon off,
(Take ribbon off.)
And tear the paper, too.
(Tear paper off.)
You see it is a birthday gift,
That I made for you.
*(Offer a pretend gift
by extending both hands.)*

Happy Birthday Song

(Tune: "She'll Be Coming 'Round the Mountain")
We'll sing happy birthday and shout hooray! (Hooray!)
We'll sing happy birthday and shout hooray! (Hooray!)
(Raise arm and shout.)
Oh, we'll sing happy birthday, we'll sing happy birthday,
We'll sing happy birthday and shout hooray! (Hooray!)

We'll light all the candles and blow whew, whew. (Whew, whew!)
(Pretend to blow out the candles.)
We'll light all the candles and we'll blow whew, whew.
(Whew, whew!)
Oh, we'll light all the candles, we'll light all the candles,
We'll light all the candles and blow whew, whew. (Whew, whew!)

We'll all eat cake and ice cream 'til we're full. (Yum, yum.)
(Rub stomach.)
We'll all eat cake and ice cream 'til we're full. (Yum, yum.)
Oh, we'll all eat cake and ice cream, we'll all eat cake and ice cream,
We'll all eat cake and ice cream 'til we're full. (Yum, yum.)

Five Birthday Candles

Five birthday candles on my special cake.
(Hold up five fingers.)
Sorry I can't tell you the wish that I'll make.
Everybody ready to sing, "Happy Birthday"?
We'll blow all the candles out and shout,
"Hooray!"
Whew, whew, whew, whew, whew, hooray!
(Blow on each finger. Hold up fist on "hooray.")

Happy Birthday

(Tune: "Sing a Song of Sixpence")
Sing out a happy birthday,
Sing it loud and clear,
Our special friend *(child's name)*
Has turned another year.
Let's stir up a special treat,
A birthday cake we'll bake,
And don't forget to light,
The candles on the cake!

Let's Move

Musical Chairs

Line up chairs (one per child) back-to-back in a row. Invite children to march around the chairs while music is playing. When the music stops, encourage children to find a chair and sit down.

Surprise Party

Ask one child to leave the room while the others hide. When the child returns, encourage everyone to jump out and shout "Surprise!"

Let's Make

Party Hats

- construction paper (12" x 18")
- stickers
- glue (colored)
- confetti
- glitter
- stapler
- ribbon strips

Invite children to decorate a sheet of construction paper with stickers. Children can then dribble colored glue over and around the stickers and sprinkle confetti and glitter on the glue. Allow the glue to dry thoroughly. Then shape each decorated sheet into a cone to fit the child's head. Carefully staple the cone together. Staple ribbon strips to each side of the party hat so children can tie the ribbons under their chins to hold the hats in place.

Birthday Cupcake Sculptures

- clay (see recipe for clay #2 on page 268)
- jar lids (one per child)
- buttons
- beads
- recycled birthday candles

Invite children to make birthday cupcakes out of various colors of clay. Encourage children to decorate their cupcakes with buttons and beads and then add candles. Place the finished cupcakes on jar lids. Allow the sculptures to air dry for several days before children take them home.

Birthday Cards

- old birthday cards
- scissors
- paper
- markers
- stickers
- stapler
- hole punch
- ribbon, glitter, rickrack, and so on
- glue

Invite children to cut up old birthday cards to create new ones. Encourage children to use a variety of materials to create unique birthday cards for friends or family members.

Let's Play

Baking-a-Cake

Props: empty cake mix boxes, measuring utensils, egg beater, styrofoam circles, birthday candles, and other baking items

Place the suggested props in the housekeeping center. Invite children to pretend to make and bake birthday cakes using the props. Children can place birthday candles in a round styrofoam circle to simulate a finished cake.

Sand Table Substitutions

Props: sand table filled with cornmeal, bowls, flour sifters, measuring spoons and cups, baker's hats, and aprons

Invite children to measure, sift, and pour cornmeal, rather than sand, at the sand table. Invite children to dress like bakers by wearing hats and aprons.

Gift Wrapping

Props: recycled gift boxes, wrapping paper, ribbons, tape, stickers, and scissors

Invite children to practice wrapping birthday gifts for family and friends using the suggested props. (Iron recycled ribbon with a warm iron to smooth out the wrinkles.)

Let's Cook

Blueberry Birthday Muffins

- blueberry muffin mix
- cream cheese (softened)
- plastic knives
- small paper plates
- birthday candles (one per child)

Invite the children to celebrate everyone's birthday. Prepare and bake the blueberry muffins as directed on the package. Cool. Give each child a muffin and a tablespoon of cream cheese to spread on it. Place a candle on the top of each child's muffin. Light one candle at a time and supervise carefully as you invite each child to make a secret wish before blowing the candles out.

Circle Time Themes

Colorful Celebrations

Children love celebrating with family and friends. The sights, sounds, and wonderful aromas that accompany such occasions provide positive lifetime memories. The themes in this section help children respond to celebrations with joy and confidence.

Marvelous Masquerade

Let's Look

Come to school in a costume. (Be sure the costume does not frighten children and be aware that many young children are frightened by masks and face paint.) Bring a suitcase filled with additional costumes to share and explore with children.

Let's Talk

- Do you like to dress up?

- What kinds of costumes do you like to wear?

- When do you wear costumes?

- How do you feel when you see someone in a clown suit? A monster suit? A princess gown?

- Are some costumes scary? Which ones?

Let's Read

Halloween Monster by Catherine Stock

Halloween Surprises by Ann Schweninger

Jillian Jiggs by Phoebe Gilman

Lion Dancer by Kate Water and Madeline Slovenz-Low

A Lion for Lewis by Rosemary Wells

Two Shoes, New Shoes by Shirley Hughes

The Very Worst Monster by Pat Hutchins

Let's Sing and Say

Who Do You See?

(Tune: "Did You Ever See a Lassie?")
Did you ever see a little child,
A little child, a little child,
Did you ever see a little child,
With glasses like this?
(Form fingers into glasses around eyes.)

Did you ever see a little child,
A little child, a little child,
Did you ever see a little child,
With a mustache like this?
(Put fingers under nose.)

Did you ever see a little child,
A little child, a little child,
Did you ever see a little child,
With a beard like this?
(Put hand on chin.)

Did you ever see a little child,
A little child, a little child,
Did you ever see a little child,
Play peek-a-boo like this?
(Cover eyes with hands, then open hands.)

Who Are You?

(Tune: "Frere Jacques")
Are you scary, are you scary?
Yes I am, yes I am.
I am a scary monster.
I am a scary monster.
Bam! Bam! Bam!
(Stomp foot.)

Are you funny, are you funny?
Yes I am, yes I am.
I am a funny clown.
I am a funny clown.
Ha! Ha! Ha!
(Imitate laughing.)

Are you fluffy, are you fluffy?
Yes I am, yes I am.
I am a fluffy bunny.
I am a fluffy bunny.
Hop! Hop! Hop!
(Hop up and down.)

My Disguise

First I put on makeup,
(Imitate putting on clown makeup.)
And then I paint my eyes.
Next I add a great big nose.
(Imitate putting on a nose.)
Can you guess my disguise?

Costumes

This little child wore a mask.
(Hold up one finger for each child.)
This little child wore a cape.
This little child wore a clown suit.
This little child wore a drape.
And this little child cried,
"Boo-hoo-hoo!"
(Rub eyes.)
I want to wear a costume, too!

Masquerade Me

(Tune: "London Bridge")
Who is behind this funny face,
Funny face, funny face?
(Make a silly face or hold up a paper mask.)
Who is behind this funny face?
Look and see, it's me.
(Remove the mask.)
Who is under this funny hat,
Funny hat, funny hat?
(Put hands on head for a hat.)
Who is under this funny hat?
Look and see, it's me.
(Remove hands.)
Who is wearing this funny cape,
Funny cape, funny cape?
(Put hands on shoulders.)
Who is wearing this funny cape?
Look and see, it's me.
(Remove hands.)

Let's Move

• **Masquerade Scarves**

Scarves make wonderful veils for beginning masquerade. (Be sensitive to the fact that some young children are frightened by covered faces.) Invite children to explore the space around them using scarves. Children can place their scarves on the floor and move around them, wave them in the air over their heads and run with them, wear them on their heads, or play "peek-a-boo." Invite children to create other movements with their scarves by covering their shoulders, waists, or parts of their faces. Play music to accompany the children's scarf movements.

Let's Make

• **Open-Face Masks**

• sturdy paper plates (one per child)

• scissors

• markers

• foil stars

• yarn scraps

• shredded paper

• long cardboard tubes (one per child)

Make non-threatening masks with the children using sturdy paper plates. Cut out the middle section of each paper plate so each child's face, or just their eyes, will show through. Invite each child to decorate his or her mask with markers, foil stars, yarn, or shredded paper. Attach a cardboard tube to the bottom of each mask for a handle. Children can use the tube to hold the mask to their faces.

Capes

- pillowcases (one per child)
- watercolor paints
- paintbrushes
- gummed stars
- colored tape
- scissors
- elastic
- safety pins

Have each child bring a plain cotton pillowcase from home. (Ask a local merchant to donate extra pillowcases for those children who are not able to bring a pillowcase from home.) Invite children to decorate their pillowcases with paint, star stickers, and colored tape. After the pillowcases are decorated and dry, cut a 6" slit on each side of each pillowcase for arm holes and an 8" neck hole along the top seam. Encourage children to wear their decorated pillowcase capes.

Let's Play

Costume Corner

Props: dance outfits, animal pajamas, hats, capes, sunglasses, wigs, and scarves

Make a costume corner by placing the dress-up props in an area of the classroom on pegs or hangers with label cards displayed over them. Invite children to come to the costume corner to experiment with different costumes and characters.

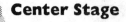

Center Stage

Props: masking tape, "microphone," sheet, clothesline, costumes, makeup mirror, dressing table, cardboard, director's chair, star chairs, and paper

Outline a stage area using masking tape. Help children use cardboard to create set designs and hang a sheet from a clothesline to make a curtain. Make a microphone by placing a small rubber or styrofoam ball on the end of a cardboard tube. Encourage children to make programs, tickets, and paper money. Then invite children to act out a story.

Let's Cook

Goofy Goggles

- refrigerator breadstick dough (1 stick per child)
- foil
- non-stick spray
- margarine (melted)
- raisins
- poppy seeds
- sesame seeds or sunflower seeds

Invite children to help make breadstick goggles. Help each child form a circle with a breadstick and place it on a foil-lined cookie sheet. Spray the foil with non-stick spray or brush with margarine. Invite each pair of children to place their circles next to each other on the tray to make a pair of eyeglasses. Connect the two circles with another strip of dough to form a nose piece. Children can brush the goggles with melted margarine and use raisins and seeds to decorate the pair of glasses. Be sure children press the decorations firmly into the dough. Bake as directed. Let the breadsticks cool and then invite children to hold the eyeglasses up to their faces and look at each other through their silly specs.

Festival of Winter Lights

Let's Look

Display a collection of holiday lights. Include a lantern, Christmas tree lights, candles, and a menorah.

Let's Talk

- Which of these lights have you seen before?
- How do you use these lights?
- Do you have these lights at your house?
- When do you use them?
- How do they work?

Let's Read

All About Hanukkah by Judye Groner

Beni's First Chanukah by Jane Zalben

Christmas Time by Catherine Stock

Everett Anderson's Christmas Coming by Lucille Clifton

Goodnight Moon by Margaret Wise Brown

Grandfather Twilight by Barbara H. Berger

Hanukkah! by Roni Schotter

Let's Play Dreidel by Roz Grossman and Gladys Gewirtz

Light by Donald Crews

The Polar Express by Chris Van Allsburg

Shadows and Reflections by Tana Hoban

Under the Sun by Ellen Kandoian

Let's Sing and Say

Starlight, Star Bright

Starlight, star bright,
First star I see tonight,
I wish I may, wish I might.
Have the wish I wish tonight.

This Little Light of Mine

This little light of mine.
*(Hold up and wave
index finger like a candle.)*
I'm gonna let it shine.
This little light of mine.
I'm gonna let it shine.
This little light of mine.
I'm gonna let it shine.
Let it shine, let it shine, let it shine.

Twinkle, Twinkle, Little Star

Twinkle, twinkle, little star.
(Open and close hands.)
How I wonder what you are!
(Open and close hands.)
Up above the world so high.
(Point to the sky.)
Like a diamond in the sky.
(Make a diamond with fingers.)
Twinkle, twinkle, little star.
(Open and close hands.)
How I wonder what you are!
(Open and close hands.)

Jack Be Nimble

Jack be nimble, Jack be quick,
Jack jump over the candlestick.

Wiggle

Wiggle fingers,
Wiggle toes,
Wiggle shoulders,
Wiggle nose.
No more wiggles
are left in me,
So I sit in my chair
as still as can be.
*(Imitate designated
movements.)*

Let's Move

• **Moonbeams**

Invite children to move around the room to music
while waving mylar ribbon or crepe-paper
streamers. Play music that inspires short, quick
movements and music that is appropriate for
slow, swaying movements. Some music suggestions
include "When You Wish Upon a Star" and
"Moonlight Sonata."

Let's Make

• Clay Candlesticks

- clay (see recipe for clay #1 on page 268)
- materials from nature, such as pinecones, twigs, pods, and so on
- small candles (one per child)

Stick a small candle (about 6") into a ball of moist clay for each child. Invite children to select nature objects and push them into the moist clay around the base of the candle. Encourage children to cover as much of the clay as possible. Let the clay candlesticks air dry for a few days. These make nice holiday gifts.

• Sparkle Wands

- small paper plates (one per child)
- foil
- shiny materials, such as gummed stars, glitter, mylar, foil, sequins, and ribbon
- glue
- tongue depressors (one per child)
- silver duct tape

Cover a small paper plate with foil for each child. Invite children to glue shiny collage materials to the foil-covered plates. Use silver duct tape to attach a foil-covered tongue depressor to each sparkling collage to make a wand.

Let's Play

• Magic Mirrors

Props: eight small plastic mirrors, duct tape, four trays, aluminum foil, counting blocks, teddy bear counters, small parquetry blocks, and small pictures

Use duct tape to hinge pairs of mirrors together. Cover four trays with aluminum foil and stand one pair of mirrors in each tray. Add a few counters and blocks. Encourage children to build with the materials inside the space between the hinged mirrors. Invite children to notice how the designs look when the mirrors are close together and how they look when the mirrors are far apart.

• Spoon Reflectors

Props: spoons of various sizes and a tray

Place the spoons on a tray and encourage children to look at their reflections in the spoons. Invite children to each take a spoon to other parts of the room. Show the children how to observe other reflections of objects around the room. Discuss the differences.

• Paper Rainbows

Props: prisms and white construction paper

Tape a piece of white paper on a wall near a window. Invite children to hold a prism near the window. Challenge children to catch the sunlight in the prism and then watch as a rainbow appears on the paper.

Let's Cook

Candlestick Salad

- pineapple rings (one per child)
- small paper plates
- bananas (1/2 per child)
- honey
- maraschino cherries (one per child)

Give each child a small paper plate and a banana. Then invite children to each place a pineapple ring in the center of his or her paper plate. Help children dip each end of their banana half in honey and place the flat end in the center of the pineapple ring. Have children place a maraschino cherry on top of the other end of the banana for the candle flame.

Spectacular Spring Eggs

Let's Look

Display a basket of colored plastic eggs. Include one hard-boiled egg and one raw egg. Open each egg and examine the insides with the children.

Let's Talk

- What do you think is inside this egg?
- Who lays eggs?
- Can you name some animals that come from eggs?
- Do you like to eat eggs?
- How do you like your eggs cooked?

Let's Read

Are You My Mother? by P.D. Eastman

Chickens Aren't the Only Ones by Ruth Heller

Egg in the Hole by Richard Scarry

An Egg Is an Egg by Nicki Weiss

The Golden Egg Book by Margaret Wise Brown

Fancy That! by Pamela Allen

It Wasn't My Fault by Helen Lester

Seven Eggs by Meredith Hooper

Let's Sing and Say

Little Chick

(Tune: "Twinkle, Twinkle, Little Star")
Little chick inside the shell,
Are you doing very well?
Can you hear me sing this song?
Must you wait there very long?
Little chick inside the egg,
Hurry up and hatch, I beg.

Pretty Eggs

Five pretty eggs in a basket by the door—
Carlos ate the red one, then there were four.
(Use names of children in classroom, if you wish.)
Four pretty eggs hidden behind a tree—
Latoya ate the green one, then there were three.
Three pretty eggs, yellow, pink, and blue—
Rose ate the yellow one, then there were two.
Two pretty eggs lying in the sun—
Peter ate the blue one, then there was one.
One pretty egg sitting by itself—
I took that pretty egg and put it on the shelf.
(Hold up five fingers, moving one finger for each verse.)

The Hungry Chickens

The first chicken said with an odd little squirm,
"I can only find this skinny little worm."
The second chicken said with a funny little shrug,
"I can only find this nasty little slug."
The third chicken said with a sharp little squeal,
"I can only find this old lemon peel."
The fourth chicken said with a little cry of grief,
"I can only find this little green leaf."
"See here," said Mother Hen from the green garden patch.
"If you want any breakfast, you come here and scratch."
(Hold up one finger for each chicken. Hold up thumb for Mother Hen.)

Humpty Dumpty

Humpty Dumpty sat on a wall;
Humpty Dumpty had a great fall.
All the king's horses
and all the king's men,
Couldn't put Humpty together again.

The Egg

(Tune: "Frere Jacques")
What do you think,
What do you think,
Is inside this egg?
Inside this egg?
Could it be a little chick?
Could it be a little chick?
Peck, peck, peck.
Peck, peck, peck.

What do you think,
What do you think,
Is inside this egg?
Inside this egg?
Could it be a little duck?
Could it be a little duck?
Quack, quack, quack.
Quack, quack, quack.

Let's Move

Chicks

Invite children to curl up on the floor and pretend to be chicks inside an egg. Encourage children to begin to roll in their eggs, slowly stretch, tap on their shells, break a hole, and finally hatch. Slowly, children can spread their wings as they dry. Then invite children to walk around like newborn chicks.

Let's Make

Colored Eggs

- sweetened condensed milk

- food coloring

- shallow containers

- sponges

- clothespins

- white construction paper

- glue

- green paint or markers

Prepare shiny pastel paints by mixing a few drops of food coloring with sweetened condensed milk. Pour the milk paint into shallow containers. Make sponge brushes by attaching small sponge squares to clothespin handles. Give each child a large egg-shaped piece of paper cut from white construction paper. Invite children to paint the oval eggs by dipping the sponges into the pastel paints and brushing or blotting color onto the paper. Children can glue their colored eggs to a larger piece of construction paper and add grass using green paint or markers.

Eggshell Collages

- hard-boiled eggs

- food coloring

- vinegar

- paper towels

- drawing paper

- glue

Invite children to help peel hard-boiled eggs and then crush the shells. (Save the hard-boiled eggs for a snack.) Soak the shells overnight in a solution of vinegar and food coloring. Spread the shells on paper towels and allow the shell pieces to dry thoroughly. Then invite children to glue pieces of shell onto small squares of paper to make eggshell collages.

Let's Play

 Egg Baskets

Props: clay and small plastic baskets

Encourage children to roll pieces of clay into egg shapes and then determine how many of their "eggs" it will take to fill a basket. Invite children to fill the baskets with clay eggs.

 Floating Eggs

Props: water table, "eggs" (plastic, rubber, hollow, solid), and pebbles

Invite children to experiment with an assortment of egg shapes to determine which eggs float on their sides and which float on their ends. Children can also fill the plastic eggs with pebbles to see how many pebbles it will take to cause an egg to sink.

Sound Eggs

Props: basket of large plastic eggs, bells, aquarium gravel, metal paper fasteners, dried beans, and tape

Fill plastic eggs with different objects to create sounds when they are shaken. Fill pairs of eggs with the same objects and seal the filled eggs with tape. Place the eggs in a basket and invite children to shake the eggs and match the pairs that sound alike.

Egg Museum

Props: eggs (wooden, plastic, marble, papier-mâché, or real eggs with the insides removed), egg cups or cartons, cardboard boxes, egg art, construction paper, and refreshments

Invite children to help create an egg museum by displaying a variety of eggs and egg shapes. Place the eggs in cups or cartons on top of display pedestals made from cardboard boxes. Display the egg art children make (eggshell collages, colored eggs) on a wall or bulletin board. Encourage children to make museum signs, such as "open" and "closed," as well as exhibit titles to display over the various eggs. Invite another class to visit the egg museum. Serve egg-shaped snacks and punch for refreshments.

Let's Cook

Excellent Eggs

- hard-boiled eggs (one per child)
- paper bowls
- plastic forks and knives
- condiments (mayonnaise, mustard, and pickle relish)
- salt
- crackers

Give each child an egg to crack and peel. Dip the egg in water to rinse. Invite children to use forks to mash their eggs in bowls. Help children add mayonnaise, mustard, salt, and pickle relish. Encourage children to spread the egg mixture on crackers and enjoy.

Pomp and Parades

Let's Look

Provide a drum and a small flag for children. Play a tape of famous marching music while you wave the flag. Pass the flag around the circle. Invite children to take turns waving the flag as you play the drum.

Let's Talk

- Where have you seen a flag?
- Where have you seen people marching and carrying flags?
- What is a parade?
- Have you ever been to a parade?
- What did you do at a parade?
- What do you see in a parade?
- Why do we have parades?

Let's Read

The Circus by Brian Wildsmith

Crash! Bang! Boom! by Peter Spier

The Fourth of July by Barbara M. Joosse

Henry's Fourth of July by Holly Keller

Parade by Donald Crews

Parade by Harriet Ziefert

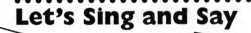

Five Little Flags

(Tune: "Lazy Mary")
I have a flag, I wave it high.
I have a flag, I wave it low.
Circle my flag
around and around,
And then I march 1, 2, 3,
Go!

Noble Duke of York

The noble Duke of York,
he had ten thousand men.
He marched them up
to the top of the hill,
And marched them down again.
(March while reciting chant.)
And when you're up, you're up,
And when you're down, you're down,
But when you're only halfway up,
You're neither up nor down!
(Imitate appropriate actions.)

Mary Mack

Miss Mary Mack, Mack, Mack
All dressed in black, black, black.
With silver buttons, buttons, buttons
Up and down her back, back, back.
She asked her mother, mother, mother
For fifty cents, cents, cents
To see the elephants, elephants, elephants
Jump off the fence, fence, fence.
They jumped so high, high, high
They touched the sky, sky, sky
And they never came back, back, back
'Til the fourth of July, July, July.

I Asked My Mother

I asked my mother
for fifty cents,
To see the elephant jump
over the fence.
He jumped so high
that he touched the sky,
And he never came back
'til the Fourth of July.

Let's Move

• Flag Parade

Choose one child to be the leader. Invite the leader to carry a flag and march around the room. Children can carry handmade flags and join in the parade. Play marching music as children parade around. Give children directions to follow, such as "wave your flag, reach it high, touch it low, put it behind you, put it in front of you, and wave it to the side."

• Tricycle Parade

Encourage children to bring their tricycles or other moving toys to school. Tape colorful paper streamers to "vehicles" and have a playground or sidewalk parade.

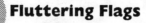

Let's Make

• Fluttering Flags

- cotton fabric

- scissors

- washable markers or crayons

- chopsticks or dowels

- glue

Cut cotton fabric into small triangles and give one to each child. Invite children to decorate the triangle flags using washable markers or crayons. Glue each completed flag to a chopstick or dowel to make a small flag. Encourage children to wave their flags in a flag parade.

• Shake-a-Shakes

- recycled plastic drink bottles (one per child)

- aquarium gravel

- gummed stars

- colored tape

Fill each plastic bottle with aquarium gravel and seal it shut. Give each child a bottle and invite children to decorate the outside of each bottle with gummed stars and bits of colored tape. Encourage children to shake their decorative bottles as they march in a parade.

Ta-Rum-Tum Drums

- oatmeal containers (one per child)

- white paper

- glue

- hole punch

- yarn

- crayons

Cover each oatmeal container with white paper and punch two holes near the top of the box (one on each side) for a neck strap. Thread heavy yarn through the holes and tie. Then invite children to decorate the drums with crayon designs. Encourage children to play their drums in a class parade.

Let's Play

 The Grand Parade

Props: chalk or tape, colorful costumes, hats, rhythm instruments, wagons, batons, and marching music

Using chalk, draw a parade line on the sidewalk or use tape to outline a path on the classroom floor. Encourage children to dress up in costumes and decorate wagons for a grand parade. Play marching music as the class follows the parade route.

 Circus Parade

Props: small toy animals, shoeboxes, collage materials, glue, and string

Encourage children to bring small toy animals to school for a circus parade. Each child can decorate a shoebox, using collage materials, to make a float on which an animal can ride in the parade. Attach a string to each float so children can pull their animals behind them as they march.

Let's Cook

Parade Pops

- bananas (1/2 per child)
- 1/2 cup honey
- 1 cup crushed oat cereal
- popsicle sticks (one per child)

Invite children to push a popsicle stick into one end of their peeled banana half. Have children dip the banana in honey and then in crushed cereal. Freeze the parade pops and serve as a post-parade treat.

Circle Time Themes

Pleasant Places

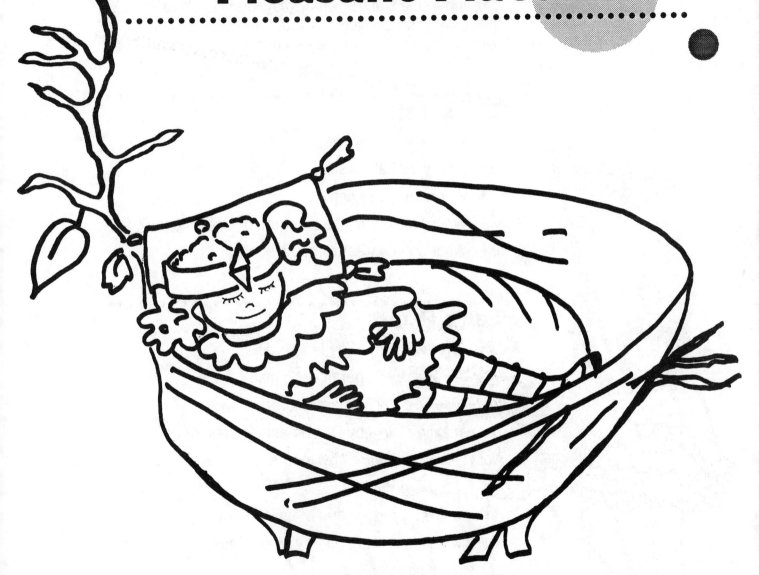

Children love intimate spaces. The spaces can be as small as a soft nest of pillows in a quiet area of the classroom or as large as a sandcastle at the beach. The themes provided here offer sensory experiences in environments enjoyed by young children.

Beds 'n Bunks

Let's Look

Make a bedroll by rolling a blanket and sheet around a pillow and tying it with a cord. During circle time, untie and roll out the bedroll. Have a canvas overnight bag and a sleeping bag on display for children to investigate as well. Demonstrate how to make a bed using doll bed linens and a doll pillow.

Let's Talk

- Where do people sleep?
- Where do babies sleep?
- Where do you sleep?
- When would you use a bedroll or sleeping bag?
- What do you wear to bed?

Let's Read

Devin's New Bed by Sally Freedman

Into the Night by Deborah Heiligman

Ira Sleeps Over by Bernard Waber

The Napping House by Donald and Audrey Wood

No Jumping on the Bed by Tedd Arnold

No Nap by Eve Bunting

Pajamas by Livingston and Maggie Taylor

Roll Over! A Counting Song by Merle Peek

Shhhh by Kevin Henkes

Ten in a Bed by Mary Rees

What Next, Baby Bear! by Jill Murphy

When I'm Sleepy by Jane R. Howard

Ten in the Bed

There were ten in the bed,
and the little one said,
"Roll over, roll over."
(Roll hands one over the other.)
And they all rolled over,
And one fell out
There were nine in the bed
And the little one said,
"Roll over, roll over."

*(Continue until there are
"none" in the bed.)*

Sleepy Fingers

My fingers are so sleepy,
it's time they went to bed.
So first you, Baby Finger,
tuck in your little head.
Ring Man, now it's your turn,
and come, Tall Man great.
Now Pointer Finger hurry,
because it's getting late.
Let's see if all are snuggled—
No, here's one more to come.
So come, lie close, little brother,
Make room for Master Thumb.
(Point to each finger as appropriate.)

Rock-a-Bye Baby

Rock-a-bye baby in the treetop.
When the wind blows, the cradle will rock.
When the bough breaks, the cradle will fall
And down will come baby, cradle and all.

Diddle, Diddle, Dumpling

Diddle, diddle, dumpling, my son John
Went to bed with his trousers on.
One shoe off and one shoe on,
Diddle, diddle, dumpling, my son John.

....
Let's Move

- ## Sheet Games

  Invite children to hold on to the edges of a spread
  bed sheet and stretch it at waist level. Direct
  children to ripple the sheet like the ocean, toss a
  teddy bear in the sheet, roll a soft ball around
  on the surface of the sheet, and finally pull the
  sheet down to rest.

- ## Nighttime

  Play a "cover up" game with a sheet. Invite children
  to sit on the floor and hold the edges of a sheet so
  it is tightly stretched. Encourage children to pull
  the covers up to their feet, over their knees, over
  their bodies, up to their chins, and finally over their
  heads to go to sleep.

Let's Make

Pretty Pillows

- white bed sheet
- scissors
- cardboard
- tape
- crayons or markers
- needle and thread (for teacher use only)
- polyester fiberfill

Recycle an old, white bed sheet for this project. Cut the sheet into 9" x 12" sections. Cut a 6" x 9" piece of cardboard for each child to use as a drawing board. Then fold the cloth over the cardboard and tape it in place. Invite children to use a colorful selection of crayons or markers to draw designs on their cloth. Be sure to write each child's name on his or her cloth. When the designs are complete, remove the cardboard. Fold each piece of cloth in half (wrong side out) and stitch around the sides, leaving a hole large enough for stuffing. Turn the pillows right side out and invite children to stuff their own pillows with fiberfill. Glue or sew the openings shut. These pretty pillows make wonderful gifts.

Snuggle Babies

- clean socks
- cotton or polyester fiberfill
- yarn
- large, plastic darning needles
- felt

Invite children to fill socks with cotton or polyester fiberfill. Using yarn, tie off the toe portions of the socks to make heads. Tie or sew the bottom of each sock together. Thread large, plastic darning needles with bright yarn. Tie the thread to the needle eye so it won't slip out and tie a piece of felt to the other end of the yarn so it won't pull through. Invite children to pull the yarn in and out of the filled sock making stitchery designs.

Let's Play

Bedtime

Props: pajamas, pillows, blankets, small suitcases, teddy bears or other soft animals, small table lamp (cord removed), bedtime stories, slippers, and robes

Add the props to the housekeeping center and encourage children to role-play preparing for bed.

Babies to Bed

Props: baby dolls, cradles, bed linens, rocking chair, doll pajamas, and bottles

Encourage children to rock the babies in rocking chairs or cradles, sing lullabies, and tuck the babies into bed. Place a basket of books near the doll beds and encourage children to "read" the babies bedtime stories.

Brush Away

Props: toothbrushes, toothpaste, and plastic cups

Encourage children to practice brushing their teeth before bedtime.

Camping Out

Props: small tent, sleeping bags, pillows, flashlights, and overnight bags or backpacks filled with pajamas

Invite children to use the props listed to pretend they are on a camping trip.

Let's Cook

Wake-Up Snack

- wheat bread (1 slice per child)
- honey butter
- plastic knives
- small paper plates
- paper cups
- fruit juice

Invite children to spread honey butter over their bread. Serve with fruit juice.

Happy Homes

Let's Look

Display pictures of different kinds of homes. Set up a doll house in the circle area. If you don't have one, make a large drawing of a house on posterboard. Give each child a paper bag with a piece of furniture or a picture of furniture in it. Invite children to match the furniture in their bags with the appropriate rooms in the house. Be sensitive to each child's living situation.

Let's Talk

- In what room of your home do you eat your meals?
- In what rooms do you play, watch TV, take a bath, and wash your clothes?
- What do you find inside houses and apartments?
- Do you live in a house, an apartment, a boat, or a mobile home?
- What are homes made of?

Let's Read

Goldilocks and the Three Bears by Jan Brett

The House That Jack Built by Elizabeth Falconer

In Our House by Anne Rockwell

My Kitchen by Harlow Rockwell

The Napping House by Audrey and Don Wood

There's No Place Like Home by Marc Brown

Three Little Pigs by Paul Galdone

The Village of Round and Square Houses by Ann Grifalconi

The House

This is the roof of the house so good.
(Hold up hands, palms facing, and slant fingers to touch fingertips.)
These are the walls that are made of wood.
(Extend hands parallel.)
These are the windows that let in the light.
(Make a square by extending index fingers up, thumbs out.)
This is the door that shuts so tight.
(Make a bigger square.)
This is the chimney so straight and tall.
(Raise index finger.)
What a good house for us, one and all!
(Hold out fingers parallel to each other.)

Two Little Houses

Two little houses all closed up tight,
(Hold up two fists.)
Open up the windows and let in the light.
(Open fists.)

The Very Nicest Place

The fish lives in the brook.
The bird lives in the tree.
But home's the very nicest place
For a little child like me.

Do You Live?

(Tune: "Frere Jacques")
Do you live, do you live,
In a house, in a house?
Does it have windows,
does it have windows?
And a door, and a door?

Do you live, do you live,
In an apartment, in an apartment?
Does it have windows,
does it have windows?
And a door, and a door?

Houses

Here is the nest for robin.
(Cup hands together.)
Here is a hive for the bee.
(Make a fist.)
Here is a hole for the bunny.
(Finger and thumb touch to make a circle.)
And here is a house for me!
(Hold up hands, palms facing, and slant fingers to touch fingertips.)

Knock at the Door

Knock at the door,
(Tap forehead.)
Peep in.
(Point to eyes.)
Lift the latch,
(Tap end of nose.)
Walk in.
(Open mouth, fingers walking towards mouth.)

Let's Move

Moving Day

Give each group of four or five children a cardboard box. Invite children to pretend they are moving by "packing" the box and carrying it around the room. Play music while the children are moving. When the music stops, direct children to sit down beside their boxes, in front of their boxes, behind their boxes, inside their boxes, or under their boxes.

••••••••••••••••••••••••••••••••••••

Let's Make

House Sculptures

- cardboard

- small boxes

- glue

Give each child a 9" x 12" piece of cardboard. Invite children to build house sculptures on their cardboard bases by gluing several small boxes together. Empty boxes from household products, such as toothpaste or aspirin, work well for this activity.

Buildings

- boxes (assorted sizes)

- construction paper

- scissors

- tape

- glue

- tempera paint

- paintbrushes

Encourage children to each choose a box and decorate it as a house. Children can use smaller boxes to add details. For example, toothpaste boxes make great chimneys. Invite children to paint their creations. Then display the houses around the classroom.

Let's Play

Moving Day

Props: cardboard boxes, newspapers, small wagon, toys, and caps

Invite children to wrap, pack, and load toys from the housekeeping center into a wagon. When all the packing is done, children can return the toys to the housekeeping center and unpack them.

The Three Pigs

Props: story character puppets, bundles of sticks, straw, cardboard bricks, and three cardboard boxes

Read or tell a version of "The Three Little Pigs." Encourage children to act out the story using the suggested props. Cut a door out of each cardboard box to make the pigs' houses.

Doll Houses

Props: doll house, furniture, family-member figures, and a toy truck

Invite children to pretend the doll family is moving and to help them pack and transport their belongings.

Let's Cook

Toast Houses

- white bread (1 1/2 slices per child)
- food coloring
- milk
- cotton swabs
- foil
- liquid margarine
- plastic knives

Give each child a whole slice of bread and a half slice cut in a triangle shape. Invite children to place the bread slices on pieces of foil. Have children place the triangular pieces on top of the whole slices to form roofs for their bread houses. Then add food coloring to small amounts of milk. Encourage children to "paint" their bread houses by dipping cotton swabs into the colored milk and drawing on the bread. Children can paint windows and other details. Place the bread houses in a toaster oven and toast until the bread crisps and colors brighten. Help children squeeze and spread a small amount of margarine on their cooked houses and then enjoy their treats.

Nice Nests

Let's Look

Place a bird's nest in a shoebox and then replace the cover. Cut a hole, about 1 inch in diameter, in one end of the box. Pass the box around the circle inviting each child to look inside.

Let's Talk

- Who lives in nests?

- Who builds nests?

- How do birds build nests?

- Do you think all nests are alike?

- Why do birds build nests?

- Could you live in a nest?

- Who else lives in nests?

Let's Read

Are You My Mother? by P.D. Eastman

Best Nest by P.D. Eastman

Hatch, Egg, Hatch: Touch and Feel Action Flap Book by Shen Roddie

My Spring Robin by Anne Rockwell

The Nest by Brian Wildsmith

What Is a Bird? by Ron Hirschi

The Little Bird

Once I saw a little bird,
Come hop, hop, hop.
So I cried, "Little bird
Will you stop, stop, stop?"
And was going to the window
To say, "How do you do?"
But he shook his little tail,
And far away he flew.

Sing a Song of Sixpence

Sing a song of sixpence,
a pocket full of rye,
Four and twenty blackbirds
baked in a pie;
When the pie was opened,
the birds began to sing.
Wasn't that a dainty dish
to set before the king?

The king was in his counting house
counting out his money.
The queen was in the parlor
eating bread and honey.
The maid was in the garden
hanging out the clothes.
Along came a blackbird
and landed on her nose!

The Robin

The north wind doth blow,
And we shall have snow.
And what will poor robin do then,
Poor thing?
He'll sit in a barn,
And keep himself warm,
And hide his head under his wing,
Poor thing.

Two Little Blackbirds

Two little blackbirds sitting on a hill.
(Hold up each fist with thumbs pointed up.)
One named Jack, one named Jill.
(Wiggle one thumb, then the other.)
Fly away Jack, fly away Jill.
(Flutter each away behind back.)
Come back Jack, come back Jill.
(Fly thumbs back into position.)

Who Lives in a Nest?

(Tune: "Did You Ever See a Lassie?")
Oh who lives in a nest, a nest, a nest?
Oh who lives in a nest?
Can you name one?
(Pause and let children provide a name.)
A bird lives in a nest, a nest, a nest.
A bird lives in a nest.
Now name one more.
(Continue adding verses about hornets,
wasps, and other nest-dwelling creatures.)

Robin Redbreast

Little Robin Redbreast sat upon a rail,
Niddle, naddle went his head.
(Nod fist for a head.)
Wiggle, waggle went his tail.
(Wiggle fingers for a tail.)

Let's Move

- **Making a Nest**

Invite children to join hands forming a circle. Choose
two children to weave crepe-paper streamers in, out,
and around the circle until all children have been
covered. Then invite children to pretend they are baby
birds in a nest. Challenge the baby birds to break out
of the nest by breaking the crepe-paper streamers
and then pretending to fly away.

Let's Make

Clay Nests

- clay (see recipe for clay #2 on page 268)
- nature materials (straw, string, dried leaves and flowers, and twigs)

Give each child a ball of clay. Invite children to stick their thumbs into the balls to form a hole. Encourage children to continue enlarging the thumb hole until they make the ball of clay into the shape of a nest. Then children can press nature materials into their clay nests. Let the nests air dry for several days.

Let's Play

Big Bird's Nest

Props: small plastic wading pool, pillows, and blankets

Invite children to pretend that the empty wading pool is a nest. Encourage children to prepare the big nest with soft pillows and blankets. Invite 2 or 3 children at a time to sit in the nest. Then have children pretend that they are birds in a nest.

Observing Nests

Props: abandoned bird nests

Display bird nests in your discovery center. Invite children to closely observe the nests. Remind children to look at, but not handle, the fragile nests.

Let's Cook

Most Delicious Nests

- peanut-butter chips
- chow mein noodles
- yogurt-covered raisins
- waxed paper

Melt peanut-butter chips and pour the melted chips over chow mein noodles to coat them. After the noodles have cooled a bit, give each child a mound of coated noodles on a sheet of waxed paper. Invite children to shape the noodles into a nest. Children can add yogurt-covered raisins to represent eggs in their noodle nests.

Beautiful Beaches

Let's Look

Place a small wading pool, half full of sand, in the center of your circle. Bury seashells and driftwood in the sand and provide shovels and buckets. Invite children to dig for "treasures" in the sand.

Let's Talk

- What is sand?

- Where do you usually see sand?

- Have you ever been to the beach?

- Where does sand come from?

- What can you do with sand?

- What happens when sand gets wet?

Let's Read

At the Beach by Anne and Harlow Rockwell

Beach by Susan Baum

Beach Day by Helen Oxenbury

Down at the Bottom of the Deep Dark Sea by Rebecca C. Jones

Just Grandma and Me by Mercer Mayer

One Sun by Bruce McMillan

The Seaside Picture Book by H. Amery

Going to the Beach

(Tune: "London Bridge")
Merrily we ride along,
ride along, ride along,
Merrily we ride along,
going to the beach.

I hope we get there very soon,
very soon, very soon.
I hope we get there very soon,
I can hardly wait.

When we're there we'll run and play,
run and play, run and play.
When we're there we'll run and play,
I can hardly wait.

Five Little Seashells

Five little seashells sleeping on the shore—
(Hold up five fingers, bending down one finger for each verse.)
Swish! went a big wave, and then there were four.
(Move arms, palms up, to make the waves.)
Four little seashells quiet as can be—
Swish! went a big wave, and then there were three.
Three little seashells pearly and new—
Swish! went a big wave, and then there were two.
Two little seashells lying in the sun—
Swish! went a big wave, and then there were none.
Five little seashells gone out to sea,
(Point out to the sea.)
Wait until morning and they'll return to me.
(Point to self.)

A Sailor Went to Sea, Sea, Sea

A sailor went to sea, sea, sea,
To see what he could see, see, see,
But all that he could see, see, see,
Was the bottom of the deep blue
sea, sea, sea!

The Sea

Behold the wonders of the mighty deep,
Where crabs and lobsters learn to creep,
And little fishes learn to swim,
And clumsy sailors tumble in.

Let's Move

Beach Buddies

Divide the class into pairs. Invite children to pretend they are playing at the beach with their buddies as they sing the song to the right.

Little Drops of Water

Little drops of water,
Little grains of sand
Make the mighty ocean
And the pleasant land.

Fun at the Beach

(Tune: "Here We Go 'Round the Mulberry Bush")
This is the way we dig in the sand.
(Pretend to dig.)
Dig in the sand, dig in the sand.
This is the way we dig in the sand,
So early in the morning.

This is the way we play in the surf,
(Pretend to run in and out of the water.)
Play in the surf, play in the surf.
This is the way we play in the surf,
So early in the morning.

This is the way we lie in the sun,
(Lie on back.)
Lie in the sun, lie in the sun.
This is the way we lie in the sun,
So early in the morning.

Let's Make

Seascapes

- shallow trays

- fingerpaint (see recipes for fingerpaint on page 268)

- paper cups

- plastic spoons

- recording of ocean sounds

- white drawing paper

- bucket of clean water

- towels

Give each child a shallow tray and small cups of green, blue, and white fingerpaint. Encourage children to spoon the paints onto their trays and move the paints around with their hands and fingers. Play a recording of ocean sounds as children create their seascapes. After a design is completed in the tray, help children press a piece of white drawing paper over the wet paint to transfer the design onto the paper. Instruct children to carefully lift the paper from the tray to preserve the design. Have a bucket of clean water handy and towels nearby for cleanup.

Sand Casts

- glue

- sand

- water

- plastic tubs

- cardboard

- seashells, driftwood, cork, and sea salt

Help the children combine small amounts of glue, water, and sand in plastic tubs until the mixture is the consistency of oatmeal. Children can place a mound of the sand mixture on a cardboard base (8" x 8") and mold the mixture with their hands. Encourage children to press small seashells, driftwood, cork, or sea salt into their wet sand sculptures. Allow several days for the sand casts to dry before the children take them home.

Let's Play

• Sand Fun

Props: sand table and beach toys

Invite children to use beach toys at the sand table for some indoor sand fun.

• Beach Day

Props: towels, sunglasses, swimsuits, beach umbrella, stool, empty sunscreen bottles, thongs, books, shovels, pails, and beach balls

Encourage children to help collect beach props to add to the drama center. Invite children to sit or lie on their beach towels while one child sits on a big stool and pretends to be a lifeguard. Children can pretend to build sandcastles or role-play other beach activities, too.

•••••••••••••••••••••••••••••••••••••••
Let's Cook

Sand and Shells

- shell-shaped macaroni (cooked)
- margarine (softened)
- Parmesan cheese (grated)
- small paper cups

Give each child a small cup of cooked macaroni shells. Help children stir in 1 tablespoon of margarine. Then have children sprinkle their buttered macaroni with 1 tablespoon Parmesan cheese. Enjoy the sand and shell snacks with the children.

Circle Time Themes
Creepy Critters

Children are fascinated with small creatures. With a mixture of awe and trepidation, children observe their habits from near and far. The themes in this section mix wonder and whimsy to help children understand and appreciate the smallest of animals.

Clever Caterpillars

Let's Look

If possible, display a jar of live caterpillars for children to observe. Or, display a collection of caterpillar photographs or pictures from magazines and books.

Let's Talk

- Have you ever seen a caterpillar?
- How do caterpillars move?
- Do caterpillars have eyes, ears, and legs?
- What do caterpillars eat?
- What special thing happens to caterpillars?

Let's Read

Butterfly by Paula Hogan

Darkness and the Butterfly by Ann Grifalconi

From Egg to Butterfly by Marlene Reidel

House of Leaves by Kiyoshi Soya

If At First You Do Not See by Ruth Brown

The Little Green Caterpillar by Yvonne Hooker

Monarch Butterfly by Gail Gibbons

The Very Hungry Caterpillar by Eric Carle

Where Butterflies Grow by Joanne Ryder

Worms Wiggle by David Pelham

Let's Sing and Say

The Caterpillars

(Tune: "London Bridge")
Caterpillars crawl around, crawl around, crawl around.
Caterpillars crawl around, down on the ground.
Caterpillars climb up high, climb up high, climb up high.
Caterpillars climb up high, looking for some food.
Caterpillars find a leaf, find a leaf, find a leaf.
Caterpillars find a leaf, to eat for a snack.
Caterpillars spin around, spin around, spin around.
Caterpillars spin around, making a cocoon.
Caterpillars stay inside, stay inside, stay inside.
Caterpillars stay inside, all winter long.
In the spring they wake right up, wake right up, wake right up.
In the spring they wake right up, with wet and shiny wings.
Now they are pretty moths, pretty moths, pretty moths.
Now they are pretty moths, and soon they'll fly away.

Caterpillar

Caterpillar, caterpillar,
brown and furry,
(Move cupped hand
along arm.)
Winter is coming
and you'd better hurry.
(Move hand faster.)
Find a leaf
under which to creep.
(Hold one hand
over cupped hand.)
Spin a cocoon
in which to sleep.
(Spin hand 'round and
'round cupped hand.)
Then when springtime
comes one day,
(Open arms in a large
circular motion.)
You'll be a moth
and fly away!
(Hook thumbs and wave
hands in a flying motion.)

Let's Move

• Caterpillars

Invite children to crawl around like caterpillars. Children can then pretend to attach to a twig, spin a cocoon, and hold on during rain, wind, and snow. Then the warm sun shines and the "caterpillars" can slowly come out of their chrysalis, move their wet new wings, and fly like moths.

Let's Make

• Caterpillar Puppets

- cotton socks or stockings (one per child)

- yarn

- buttons

- colored cotton balls

- pipe cleaners
- ribbon
- glue

Invite children to glue a variety of materials on cotton socks or stockings to make caterpillars. Push both ends of a pipe cleaner through the toe of each sock to make antennae. Children can wear the socks as caterpillar arm puppets.

Caterpillar Sculptures

- clay (see recipe for clay #2 on page 268)
- plastic bags
- chenille stems
- small buttons
- cardboard

Prepare clay in four different colors. Place the cooled dough in plastic bags. Give each child a 6" square of cardboard. Invite children to choose pieces of dough and make balls from the dough for caterpillar segments. Show the children how to push two small buttons into the heads of their caterpillars to make eyes and pieces of chenille stem in the dough to make antennae. Let the caterpillars air dry and display around the classroom.

Caterpillar Communities

- butcher paper
- glue
- colored cotton balls
- collage materials (paper scraps, leaves, twigs)

Invite children to each glue 5 or 6 cotton balls in a row on a large sheet of butcher paper to make caterpillars. Children can glue collage materials around the crawling critters to make caterpillar communities.

Let's Play

Caterpillar Play

Props: sweatbands with pipe cleaner antennae attached and old sheets or curtains

Invite children to wear antennae sweatbands and pretend to be caterpillars. Children can pretend to spin a cocoon. Encourage children to use sheets or curtains to make moth wings as they emerge from their cocoons.

Scientists

Props: fresh leaves, terrarium, and caterpillars

Prepare a terrarium for tent caterpillars. Give the caterpillars a supply of fresh leaves daily. Invite children to observe the caterpillars spinning cocoons. Place a drop of water on the cocoons every day or two. Over time, children can observe the moths emerging from their cocoons.

Let's Cook

Caterpillar Biscuits

- refrigerator biscuits (2 per child)
- sesame seeds
- poppy seeds
- grated cheese
- pretzel sticks
- raisins
- butter or margarine (melted)

Prepare small bowls of sesame seeds, poppy seeds, and grated cheese. Give each child two biscuits and invite children to form four small dough balls. Help children dip the dough balls in melted butter and then roll them in seeds or cheese. Encourage children to press the balls together to form a caterpillar. Then bake the biscuits according to the directions on the package. When the caterpillar biscuits are done, children can spear raisins on the ends of two pretzel sticks and press them into the heads of their biscuit caterpillars for antennae.

Spindly Spiders

Let's Look

Display pictures of spiders, spider webs, and egg sacks. If possible, bring in a real web or spider in a jar. If real spiders can't be found, use rubber ones for display and discussion.

Let's Talk

- What are spiders?

- How do spiders look, feel, and move?

- How many legs do spiders have?

- Do spiders make good pets? Why or why not?

- Should you pick up spiders? (Warn children not to play with or pick up spiders.)

Let's Read

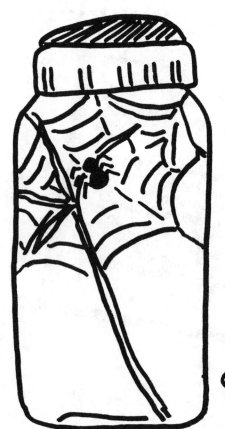

Anansi the Spider: A Tale from the Ashanti by Gerald McDermott

Backyard Insects by Millicent E. Selsam

I Know an Old Lady by Maxie Chambliss

Quick as a Cricket by Audrey Wood

Rosie Sips Spiders by Alison Lester

The Very Busy Spider by Eric Carle

Spin Little Spider

(Tune: "Farmer in the Dell")
Spin little spider, spin.
(Spin around.)
Spin little spider, spin.
'Round and 'round
and up and down,
Spin little spider, spin.

Crawl little spider, crawl.
(Crawl around.)
Crawl little spider, crawl.
'Round and 'round
and up and down,
Crawl little spider, crawl.

Dance little spider, dance.
(Dance around.)
Dance little spider, dance.
'Round and 'round
and up and down,
Dance little spider, dance.

Eensy, Weensy Spider

The eensy, weensy spider
went up the water spout.
(Make climbing motion with fingers.)
Down came the rain
and washed the spider out.
(Motion hands downward and out.)
Out came the sun
and dried up all the rain.
(Form a circle with arms overhead.)
The eensy weensy spider
went up the spout again.
(Repeat climbing motion.)

Let's Sing and Say

Little Miss Muffet

Little Miss Muffet sat on a tuffet,
eating her curds and whey.
Along came a spider and
sat down beside her,
And frightened Miss Muffet away.

The Spider

(Tune: "Twinkle, Twinkle Little Star")
There's a spider on the wall.
If he's careful he won't fall.
He moves slowly down the wall.
I can watch him crawl and crawl.
I wonder if he minds my stare,
Or does he know and just not care.

Let's Move

- **Spiders**

Invite children to move like spiders in tight little egg
sacks, building webs, and dangling from invisible
cords. Encourage children to form giant webs as
they unwind balls of black yarn while they move in,
under, and around furniture in the classroom.

Let's Make

- **Spindly Spiders**

- small styrofoam balls

- egg cartons

- cotton balls

- pipe cleaners

- paper strips

- colored toothpicks

- elastic cord

- fishing net (optional)

First Time Circle Time

Discuss with children what spiders look like. Help children think of ways that they can use the collected materials to make spindly spider sculptures. Do not provide models. String the finished sculptures on elastic cords and hang them from the ceiling or in a fishing net.

• Transparent Webs

- clear plastic wrap or laminating paper
- black crayons or markers

Cover a window with pieces of clear plastic wrap or laminating paper. Invite children to use black crayons to draw random dots on the plastic. Then have children connect the dots to make spider webs.

Let's Play

• Spider Rescue

Props: water table, rubber or plastic spiders, and metal tongs

Invite children to use metal tongs to "rescue" spiders from the water. Children can dump the spiders back into the water after each rescue to continue playing.

• Wonder Webs

Props: rubberbands, black yarn, geoboards, and small rubber or plastic spiders

Invite children to create "wonder webs" by stringing yarn and stretching rubberbands across and through the geoboard pegs. Children can add small rubber or plastic spiders to their completed webs. Be sure children disassemble their creations to leave the center ready for the next web builders.

Web Play

Props: large fishing net and a table

Spread a large fishing net over a table to create a huge web. Invite children to crawl into the web (under the table) and pretend to be friendly spiders.

Let's Cook

Curds and Whey

- cottage cheese
- pineapple chunks
- peach or pear slices
- small bowls
- plastic spoons

Give each child a small bowl of cottage cheese (curds and whey). Invite children to add fruit (pineapple, peaches, pears) and enjoy. Encourage children to act out the Little Miss Muffet nursery rhyme, if they wish.

Freckled Frogs

Let's Look

Before circle time, make a large, green lily pad from construction paper and a green headband with frog eyes for each child. Use a frog puppet to welcome children to the circle. Invite children to wear their frog headbands while sitting on their lily pads.

Let's Talk

- What do you know about frogs?
- Where do frogs live?
- How do frogs move?
- What do frogs eat?
- What sounds do frogs make?

Let's Read

The Caterpillar and the Polliwog by Jack Kent

Frog Went a Courtin' by John Langstaff and Feodor Rojankovsky

Jump, Frog, Jump! by Robert Kalin

Mushroom in the Rain by Miriam Ginsburg

The Mysterious Tadpole by Steven Kellogg

One Green Frog by Yvonne Hooker

Over in the Meadow by Paul Galdone

Wide-Mouthed Frog by Rex Schneider

Let's Sing and Say

Frog Songs

One little frog is singing in a tree.
Ba-rum, ba-rum, ba-ree.
Two little frogs sing by my door.
Ba-rum, ba-rum, ba-roar.
Three little frogs on a rock in the creek.
Ba-rum, ba-rum, ba-reak.
Four little frogs singing on a log,
Ba-rum, ba-rum, ba-rogg.
Five little frogs singing through the night.
When the morning sun comes up
they all hop out of sight.
(Hold up the appropriate number of fingers.
Hide hand at "hop.")

Five Funny Speckled Frogs

Five funny speckled frogs sat on a spotted log,
(Hold out arm for a log and place
five fingers of other hand on top.)
Eating the most delicious bugs. Yum! Yum!
(Rub tummy.)
One jumped into a pool, where it was nice and cool.
(Jump with hand into a pool and return hand
with the appropriate number of fingers for each verse.)
Then there were four funny speckled frogs.

Additional Verses:
Four funny speckled frogs...
Three funny speckled frogs...
Two funny speckled frogs...

Final Verse:
One funny speckled frog sat on a spotted log,
Eating the most delicious bugs. Yum! Yum!
He jumped into the pool, where it was nice and cool,
Then there were no more speckled frogs!

I Wish I Were a Little Frog

(Tune: "Put Your Fingers in the Air")
Oh, I wish I were a little green frog. Glub, glub!
I wish I were a little green frog. Glub, glub!
I wish I were a frog, just sittin' on a log.
I wish I were a little green frog. Glub, glub!

Oh, I wish I were a little brown toad. Gluck, gluck!
I wish I were a little brown toad. Gluck, gluck!
I wish I were a toad, a hoppin' cross a road.
I wish I were a little brown toad. Gluck, gluck!

The Frog Song

(Tune: "Twinkle, Twinkle Little Star")
Froggie, Froggie, I hear you
Singing in the lake so blue.
Rivet, rivet, croak, croak, croak
Rivet, rivet, croak, croak, croak
Froggie, Froggie, I hear you
Singing in the lake so blue.

Over in the Meadow

Over in the meadow,
in the sand, in the sun
Lived an old mother frog
and her little froggie one.
"Croak," said the mother.
"I croak" said the one,
And they croaked
and they croaked
in the sand in the sun.

Let's Move

Hoppin' Frogs

Place construction-paper lily pads (one per child) around the room. Play some appropriate music and invite children to hop like frogs. When the music stops, have children hurry to a lily pad and sit down.

Let's Make

● **Pond Prints**

  ● fingerpaint (green and blue)

  ● fingerpaint paper

  ● green tissue paper

  ● confetti

Invite children to make fingerpaintings with green and blue fingerpaint. Encourage children to create pond prints by adding green tissue paper and colorful confetti to the wet paintings.

● **Chalk Ponds**

  ● empty water table

  ● pan of water

  ● colored chalk

  ● drawing paper

Place a pan of water in the center of the empty water table. Invite each child to dip a sheet of paper into the water and then hold the paper over the pan to allow the excess water to drip off. Then invite children to place their wet paper on a table and draw on the paper with colored chalk.

Let's Play

● **Pond Playground**

Props: water table, blue or green food coloring, green sponges, rocks, rubber frogs, ducks, snakes, and flowers

Fill the water table with blue or green water. Float green sponges in the water to represent lily pads. Children can use the props to create their own pond playground using the props listed.

Raising Tadpoles

Props: frog eggs, fish bowl or aquarium, pond water, algae, and cornmeal

In early spring, look for frog eggs in streams and ponds (or order frog eggs from a science supplies distributor). Carefully remove a few with a soft net and place them in a fish bowl or aquarium. Fill the fish bowl with pond water. Provide algae and a small amount of cornmeal for the tadpoles to eat. Invite children to observe the eggs and the changes the eggs go through as they develop. As the legs start to appear, return the frogs to their natural habitat. Note: It is extremely difficult to raise tadpoles in captivity.

Let's Cook

Lily-Pad Floats

- lime sherbet
- lemonade
- plastic cups
- plastic spoons
- drinking straws

Help each child place a small scoop of lime sherbet in the bottom of a cup. Fill each cup with lemonade. Encourage children to enjoy their floats by sipping through a straw.

Bumbly Bees

Let's Look

Invite a beekeeper to visit your class. Encourage children to look closely at his or her special suit, helmet, gloves, and beehives. Examine a piece of honeycomb. If a beekeeper is not available, display a collection of bee and beehive pictures for the children.

Let's Talk

- Who makes honey?
- How do bees make honey?
- What else do bees do?
- What do bees eat?
- Why do bees buzz?

Let's Read

Bugs by Nancy Winslow Parker and Joan R. Wright

Bugs! by Patricia McKissack

From Blossom to Honey by Ali Mitgutsch

The Grouchy Ladybug by Eric Carle

Rosie's Walk by Pat Hutchins

The Very Quiet Cricket by Eric Carle

What's in Fox's Sack? by Paul Galdone

First Time Circle Time

Busy Bee

(Tune: "Row, Row, Row Your Boat")
Buzz, buzz, buzzy bee,
Buzzing all around.
Lighting on the clover,
Lighting on the ground.

Biz, biz, busy bee,
Working all day long.
Never time to take a break,
Or stop your busy song.

I Eat My Peas with Honey

I eat my peas with honey;
I've done it all my life.
It makes the peas taste funny,
But it keeps them on the knife.

Little Peter Rabbit

(Tune: "Battle Hymn of the Republic")
Little Peter Rabbit
had a bee upon his nose.
Little Peter Rabbit
had a bee upon his nose.
Little Peter Rabbit
had a bee upon his nose.
And he twitched it
'til it buzzed away.

Little Peter (rabbit motion)
had a bee upon his nose.
(Make rabbit-ears motion
instead of saying "rabbit.")
Little Peter (rabbit motion)
had a bee upon his nose.
Little Peter (rabbit motion)
had a bee upon his nose.
And he twitched it
'til it buzzed away.

(Continue the song, substituting
motions for words:
touching nose for "nose,"
making a buzzing sound for bee,
wiggling nose for "twitches,"
and waving arms and buzzing
for "buzzed" away.)

Let's Move

Bumblebees

Discuss with children how bees move. Encourage children to suggest ways they could imitate these movements. Play a recording of "Flight of the Bumblebee" while children move around the classroom like busy bees in clover. Encourage children to pretend they are flying in a swarm, making honey in the hive, and gathering nectar from flowers.

Let's Make

Honeycombs

- sponges

- clothespins

- drawing paper

- yellow tempera paint in shallow pans

- corncobs (optional)

Clip small sponge squares to clothespins to make sponge paintbrushes. Invite children to dip the sponges into tempera paint and create honeycomb textured prints on drawing paper. Corncobs rolled in paint and then on drawing paper also make nice honeycomb prints as well.

Bumblebee Wings

- white sheet

- crayons

- scissors

- pipe cleaners

Cover a large table with a white sheet. Place a basket of crayons on the table. Encourage children to draw lines on the cloth. When complete, cut the fabric into 10" x 12" rectangles. Wrap a pipe cleaner around the center of each rectangle to make wings. Attach the wings to each child's back and invite children to be bees for a day.

• Antennae Hats

- construction paper
- fluorescent tempera paints
- cotton swabs
- pipe cleaners, cardboard, or wooden ice-cream spoons
- glue
- stapler
- small pom-poms

Cut construction paper into 3" x 14" strips. Give each child two strips stapled together at the ends. Invite children to dip cotton swabs in fluorescent paint and make random dots all over the long paper strips. When the strips are dry, help children glue two pipe cleaners, cardboard strips, or wooden ice-cream spoons to the fronts of their headbands for antennae. Children can glue pom-poms to the ends of each antennae as well. Carefully staple the paper strips to fit around each child's head.

Let's Play

• Clover-Patch Farmers

Props: gallon milk cartons, potting soil, clover seeds, and clay pot or window box

Cut gallon milk cartons in half and help each child fill one with potting soil. Invite children to pretend to be clover-patch farmers by sprinkling seeds on the surface of the soil. Invite children to water their gardens and place them in a sunny window. Encourage children to observe the clover seeds as they begin to sprout. When the plants are two inches tall, transplant them into a large clay pot or window box. In early spring, divide the clover patch up and give each child a clump of clover to take home and plant in his or her backyard for the bees.

Beehive Builders

Props: masking tape and blocks

Using masking tape, make a large honeycomb design on the carpet in the block center. Invite children to stack blocks within the marked areas to build a honeycomb.

Let's Cook

Beehive Waffles

- 1 cup whole wheat flour
- 1/2 cup flour
- 1 tsp baking powder
- 1/4 tsp salt
- 1 1/2 cups milk
- 1/2 cup sour cream
- 2 Tbsp margarine (melted)
- 1 Tbsp honey
- 1 egg, lightly beaten
- cooking oil

Combine the dry ingredients. Using your hands, make a hole in the middle of the mixture. Pour the milk, sour cream, margarine, honey, and egg in the hole. Stir from the center out, mixing the ingredients into a smooth batter. Cover the bowl and let it sit for one hour. Lightly grease a waffle iron with cooking oil and then heat. Cook the waffles according to directions. Serve the beehive waffles with honey.

Circle Time Themes
Green Thumbs

Potting Soil

Children love to garden. For them, harvesting is probably the most enjoyable part. The themes in this section help children learn how things grow and change and promote exploring ways the harvest can be used.

Apple Appeal

Let's Look

Place a small picnic tablecloth on the floor and display a basket of apples, in a variety of colors, in the center. Arrange the display like a still-life fruit picture. Using a cutting board, knife (for teacher use only), and peelers, invite children to help investigate the apples.

Let's Talk

- What is an apple?

- Do all apples look alike?

- How are they different?

- How are apples used?

- What do you think is inside an apple?

- Do you like apples?

- What is your favorite apple?

Let's Read

The Apple Bird by Brian Wildsmith

Apples and Pumpkins by Anne Rockwell

How They Grow Apples by Bruce McMillan

The Season of Arnold's Apple Tree by Gail Gibbons

Where Are You Going Emma? by Jeanne Titherington

I Like Apples

(Tune: "Mary Had a Little Lamb")
I like apples big and red,
Big and red, big and red.
I like apples big and red,
They are so very juicy.

I like apples yellow bright
Yellow bright, yellow bright,
I like apples yellow bright,
They taste just delicious.

Let's Sing and Say

Growing Apples

(Tune: "Muffin Man")
Oh, do you know how apples grow,
How apples grow, how apples grow?
Oh, do you know how apples grow?
They grow on a tree!
(Substitute other foods that grow on trees.)

Dig a Little Hole

Dig a little hole.
(Imitate a digging motion.)
Plant a little seed.
(Imitate dropping a seed.)
Pour a little water.
(Imitate pouring.)
And pull a little weed.
(Imitate a pulling motion.)

Apple Tree

Way up high in an apple tree,
Two little apples smiled at me.
(Point up in the air,
smile, and touch lips.)
I shook that tree
as hard as I could,
(Imitate shaking a tree.)
Down came those apples,
Mmmmmm, they were good.
(Make a motion with arms of
falling apples and then rub tummy.)

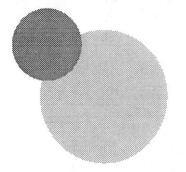

Let's Move

- **Apple Trees**

Invite children to pretend to be apple trees by
standing with their arms overhead. Say "We are
apple trees so very tall. See our finger leaves move
in the breeze. (Move fingers.) Warm raindrops give
us summer showers. (Move body like in the rain.)
Little winds shake us dry. (Shake gently.) In autumn,
our apples are big and round, and one by one they
fall on the ground. (Drop arms to the side.)"

Let's Make

- **Apple Prints**
  - grocery bags
  - apples
  - knife (for teacher use only)
  - paintbrushes
  - tempera paint (red, green, yellow)
  - pinking shears (for teacher use only)
  - construction paper (red, green, yellow)

Cut some apples horizontally and some vertically. Cut grocery bags into drawing-paper size pieces. Invite children to use paintbrushes to apply paint to the cut sides of apples. Have children press the painted sides of the apples on the grocery bag papers to create interesting print designs. When the prints are dry, use pinking shears to trim the edges. Mount the prints on red, green, or yellow construction paper.

Let's Play

The Amazing Apple Company

Props: plastic apples, small baskets, signs, paper bags, play money, and a cash register

Invite children to help set up a fruit stand. Encourage children to pretend to sell and buy apples using the props listed.

Planting Apple Seeds

Props: apple seeds, paper cups, and potting soil

Punch a few small holes in the bottom of each of the paper cups for drainage. Then give each child a paper cup to fill with soil. Have children use their fingers to make a hole in the soil. Children can drop two or three apple seeds into the hole. Invite children to water the planted seeds and place the cups in a sunny window. Apple seeds are very unpredictable. You may want to wrap the apple seeds in moist paper towels and leave them in the refrigerator for three months before planting to increase their chances of sprouting.

Visit an Orchard

Props: apples and recipes

If possible, arrange a visit to an apple orchard to pick apples. Return to school and plan ways to prepare the apples with the children. Apples can be sliced and cooked in an electric skillet, baked in a cobbler or pie, or stewed and mashed for applesauce.

Investigating Apples

Props: apples, scale, string, measuring tape, and baskets

Invite children to sort, weigh, and measure a variety of apples. Younger children can fill and empty baskets of apples. Plastic apples or rubber balls work best as substitutes for real apples.

Let's Cook

Cinnamon Apples

- apples (1/2 per child, core removed)
- knife (for teacher use only)
- cinnamon
- brown sugar
- margarine
- insulated paper cups
- plastic spoons

Core the apples, cut them in half, and then cut the apples into slices. Place the apple slices in an electric skillet. Invite children to help sprinkle the sliced apples with cinnamon. Stir in brown sugar and butter. Add 1 tablespoon of water. Cover and simmer until tender. Serve the cinnamon apples in insulated cups. If you are unable to cook the apples, serve the slices spread with peanut butter, cream cheese, or honey.

Forestry Fun

Let's Look

Place a collection of seasonal leaves and evergreen needles in a basket. Pass the basket around the circle and invite each child to take a leaf. Encourage children to carefully observe the leaves and describe their characteristics.

Let's Talk

- What is a leaf?
- Where do you find leaves?
- What size is a leaf?
- Are leaves smooth or rough?
- Do leaves have points?
- What color are leaves?
- What can you do with leaves?

Let's Read

The After Christmas Tree by Linda Wagner Tyler

Changes by Marjorie N. Allen

The Great Kapok Tree by Lynne Cherry

Hello, Tree! by Joanne Ryder

The Oak Tree by Jane Coats

Rain Forest by Helen Cowcher

Red Leaf, Yellow Leaf by Lois Ehlert

A Tree Is Nice by Janice Udry

Uncle Vova's Tree by Patricia Polacco

Let's Sing and Say

Trees

(Tune: "O Christmas Tree")
Oh cedar tree, oh cedar tree,
How ever green your branches.
Oh cedar tree, oh cedar tree,
How ever green your branches.
You never change the whole year 'round.
You brighten up the snowy ground.
Oh cedar tree, oh cedar tree,
How ever green your branches.

Oh tall oak tree, oh tall oak tree,
How colorful your branches.
Oh tall oak tree, oh tall oak tree,
How colorful your branches.
In spring you have new green leaves.
In summertime they blow in the breeze.
In autumn though they turn to gold,
Oh tall oak tree, I love you so.

Dancing Leaves

The autumn leaves come dancing down,
Yellow, red, gold and brown.
*(Wiggle fingers and move hands
as if floating down.)*
They make a carpet on the ground.
(Move hands as though smoothing ground.)
And fall asleep without a sound.
*(Place hands together by face
to imitate sleeping.)*

Under the Spreading Chestnut Tree

Under the spreading chestnut tree,
(Hold hands in a circle overhead.)
When I held you on my knee,
(Slap knee.)
We were as happy as could be,
(Point to smiling face.)
Under the spreading chestnut tree.
(Hold hands in a circle overhead.)
*(Sing the song again, replacing the
key words with motions.)*

Let's Move

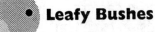

Growing Trees

Invite children to curl up on the floor in a little ball. Say "We are little seeds under the ground." Encourage children to raise one arm slowly with finger closed. Say "Up comes a shoot and some leaves." Children open their fingers and repeat the motions with their other arm. Invite children to gradually stand up as you say "And we grow, and we grow, and we grow into tall, tall trees."

Let's Make

Leafy Bushes

- pine needles
- sticks
- string or wire twist ties

Help children tie a small bundle of pine needles to the end of a stick. Children can use their leafy bushes as paintbrushes or tiny brooms.

Leaf Windows

- graters
- waxed paper
- crayons
- leaves
- tissue paper
- confetti
- iron (for teacher use only)

Use a small hand grater to grate the crayons. Give each child a sheet of waxed paper and invite children to arrange the grated crayons, leaves, tissue paper, and confetti on the waxed paper. Place another sheet of waxed paper over the top of the designs and run a warm iron over them. Display the finished work in a sunny window for see-through art.

Let's Play

Tree Hideout

Props: large cardboard appliance box and green posterboard

Cut a large opening in the front of the box. This will be the tree trunk. Attach a piece of green posterboard on top of the trunk to make a treetop. Children can crawl inside the tree hideout. This makes an excellent quiet space for children.

Tree Nursery

Props: acorns, flowerpots, soil, fruit seeds, hats, rake, hoe, and hand trowel

Plant acorns that have been soaked in water overnight in a flowerpot filled with soil. Soak the fruit seeds, such as peach or pear seeds, and plant them as well. Keep the pots watered and watch for sprouts and leaves. Encourage children to use the props to pretend they are tending a tree nursery.

Seed Sort

Props: empty sand or water table, scoops, containers, and seeds

Invite children to sort a collection of seeds at a discovery center. Fill an empty sand or water table with seeds for children to scoop. Provide small containers for children to fill with seeds and soil.

Let's Cook

Tree Treats

- 2 cups low-fat cottage cheese
- 1 tsp dried dill
- 1/4 tsp dry mustard
- 1 tsp garlic powder
- 1/4 tsp salt

- cauliflower
- broccoli
- cherry tomatoes
- shallow container or tray
- small bowls (1 for each child)

Combine the first five ingredients in a blender. Blend the mixture until smooth. Divide the mixture into small bowls, one for each child, and chill. Wash the broccoli and cauliflower and cut into small bunches. Invite children to arrange the cut vegetables and cherry tomatoes in the shape of a tree on a tray. Give each child a small bowl of dip. Encourage children to dip the vegetables in the cheese mixture for a tasty snack.

Flower Power

Let's Look

Display a bouquet of flowers in a pretty vase on a low table. Sit beside the table as you call the children to circle time.

Let's Talk

- What is a flower?
- How do flowers smell?
- Where do flowers grow?
- Where are the petals, leaves, and stem on a flower?
- How are flowers cared for?
- What do flowers need to grow?

Let's Read

First Comes Spring by Anne Rockwell

Planting a Rainbow by Lois Ehlert

The Happy Day by Ruth Kraus

The Reason for a Flower by Ruth Heller

The Rose in My Garden by Arnold and Anita Lobel

That's What Happens When It's Spring by Elaine Good

The Tiny Seed by Eric Carle

Wild Wild Sunflower Child Anna by Nancy White Carlstrom

My Garden

This is my garden. I'll rake it with care.
(Imitate raking.)
And then some flower seeds I'll plant in there.
(Imitate planting seeds.)
The sun will shine,
(Make a circle above head with hands.)
And the rain will fall,
(Flutter fingers, imitating rain.)
And my garden will blossom,
and grow straight and tall.
(Imitate flowers blooming with hands.)

White Coral Bells

White coral bells upon a slender stalk,
Lilies-of-the-valley deck my garden walk.
Oh, don't you wish
that you could hear them ring?
That only happens when the fairies sing.

Mistress Mary, Quite Contrary

Mistress Mary, quite contrary,
How does your garden grow?
With silver bells and cockleshells
And pretty maids all in a row.

The Flower

Here's a green leaf.
(Show one cupped hand.)
And here's a green leaf.
(Show other cupped hand.)
That you see makes two.
Here is a bud
that makes a flower.
(Cup hands together.)
Watch it bloom for you.
(Gradually open hands and spread fingers like a flower.)

Let's Move

- **Flowers**

Play "Waltz of the Flowers" from the Nutcracker Suite while children dance about wearing flower headbands they have made (see "Petal Headbands" on page 180).

Let's Make

- **Pastel Flowers**

  - tempera paint (blue, pink, yellow, green)

  - paintbrushes

  - drawing paper

  - "Waltz of the Flowers" recording

Invite children to paint flowers on drawing paper while you play a recording of "Waltz of the Flowers." Four-year-olds may make circular shapes. Five-year-olds can begin to draw circles with spokes for petals. Accept each child's representation of a flower.

Tissue and Starch Overlays

- tissue paper (pastel colors)

- tray

- liquid starch

- sponge brushes

- white drawing paper

Give each child a piece of tissue paper and invite children to tear the tissue into small shapes. Place the tissue shapes on a tray. Invite each child to use a sponge brush to coat a sheet of drawing paper with liquid starch. Then have children place the tissue over the starch to make collages.

Petal Headbands

- construction paper (pastel colors)

- scissors (for teacher use only)

- tissue paper

- glue

Cut a headband strip from pastel construction paper for each child. Cut tissue into small oval shapes with pointed ends to resemble petals. Then invite children to select tissue petals to glue on their headbands.

Let's Play

Flower Gardeners

Props: seeds, soil, and paper cups, peat pots or milk cartons

Invite children to help make decisions about what type of flower seeds they will plant. Give each child a paper cup, peat pot, or milk carton to fill with soil. Help children plant flower seeds in their containers and water the soil. Set each mini-flower garden in a sunny spot. When sprouts appear, follow the package directions for thinning and transplanting the plants. These flower cups make great Mother's Day or Father's Day gifts.

Garden Tools

Props: garden gloves, hats, trowels, mini-rakes, plant pots, watering can, and spray bottles

Invite children to use the props to role-play being gardeners and tending their plants.

Florists

Props: assorted artificial flowers, vases, plant pots, and clay

Encourage children to make flower arrangements. Children can place a clay base in the bottom of a flowerpot and stick artificial flower stems in the base.

Let's Cook

Flower Muffins

- English muffins (1/2 per child)
- cream cheese (softened)
- food coloring
- bowls
- raisins
- sunflower seeds

Split English muffins and toast one half for each child. Color one bowl of cream cheese with pink food coloring, another bowl with yellow, and a third bowl with blue. Fill a fourth bowl with uncolored cream cheese. Invite children to choose a color of cream cheese and help the children spread the cream cheese on their toasted muffins. Encourage children to add raisins or sunflower seeds to the center of each flower muffin for a special treat.

First Time Circle Time

Potato Planting

Let's Look

Place a tub of soil on a cloth in the middle of the circle. Bury Irish potatoes (one per child) in the soil. Invite children to guess what is in the tub. Give each child an opportunity to dig for a potato.

Let's Talk

- What do you think is in this tub?
- How are potatoes used?
- Where do potatoes grow?
- How do potatoes grow?
- How could we grow potatoes?

Let's Read

The Mouse and the Potato by Thomas Berger

Growing Vegetable Soup by Lois Ehlert

The Farmer by Rosalinda Kightley

Growing Colors by Bruce McMillen

How My Garden Grew by Anne and Harlow Rockwell

This Year's Garden by Cynthia Rylant

Let's Sing and Say

One Potato, Two Potato

One potato, two potato, three potato, four,
Five potato, six potato, seven potato, more.
(Children put fists together in a circle.
Tap each fist to the song and the child
whose fist is tapped on "more" is out.
The last fist remaining is the "hot potato.")

Potato Patch

(Tune: "Paw-Paw Patch")
Where, oh where is my friend (child's name)?
Where, oh where is my friend (child's name)?
Where, oh where is my friend (child's name)?
Way down yonder in the tater patch.

Diggin' up taters and puttin' them in a basket.
Diggin' up taters and puttin' them in a basket.
Diggin' up taters and puttin' them in a basket.
Way down yonder in the tater patch.

Farmer

First the farmer
sows her seeds.
(Imitate planting seeds.)
Then she stands
and takes her ease.
(Stand with hands on hips.)
She stamps her foot.
(Stamp foot.)
She claps her hands.
(Clap hands.)
And turns around
to view her lands.
(Turn around with hand
across eyebrows, looking.)

I Like Potatoes

(Tune: "Are You Sleeping?")
I like potatoes, I like potatoes,
Cut and fried, cut and fried.
Just add a little ketchup,
add a little ketchup,
Eat them up, eat them up.

I like potatoes, I like potatoes,
Cooked and mashed,
cooked and mashed.
Just add some milk and butter,
add some milk and butter,
Eat them up, eat them up.

I like potatoes, I like potatoes,
Wrapped and baked,
wrapped and baked.
Just add some salt and butter,
add some salt and butter,
Eat them up, eat them up.

Let's Move

● Sprouting Potatoes

Invite children to curl up like potatoes that are "sleeping" in the ground. Encourage other children to be the rain and sun. When the potatoes are ready to sprout, children can sit on the floor with their arms spread as leaves. Other children can come along and "dig" up the potatoes.

Let's Make

● Potato Prints

- tempera paint

- paintbrushes

- potatoes

- popsicle sticks

- grocery bags

- knife (for teacher use only)

- nail

Cut the grocery bags into strips. Provide shallow pans of tempera paint in a variety of colors. Cut the potatoes in half. Then encourage children to think of a simple design for their potato printers. Carve designs in the ends of the potatoes, listening carefully as each child gives you directions. Invite children to brush the potatoes with tempera paint and then stamp the potatoes onto the brown strips of paper. Discuss with children how to "walk" the designs down the strips to make printed paths.

Let's Play

Farm

Props: straw hats, caps, work gloves, overalls, work shoes, shovels, and buckets

Invite children to use the props to pretend they are working on a farm.

Potato Farm Monster

Props: plastic trash-can liner, tape, permanent markers, gravel, potting soil, Irish potatoes, and a metal tray

Using tape and permanent markers, draw a big monster face on a plastic bag. Fold the top of the bag down to form a wide ring. Fill the bottom of the bag with gravel and poke some drainage holes in the bottom and sides. Fill the bag with potting soil. Cut a couple of Irish potatoes into pieces, with "eyes" or stems showing. Plant the potato pieces in the bag monster and cover the potato pieces with more soil. Place the bag in a sunny spot on a metal tray. Keep the bag watered and wait a few months for your potato monster to grow leaves and roots. In about four months, you will be able to dig out your potatoes.

Potato Pickers

Props: baskets, plastic buckets, and potatoes

Invite children to fill and empty containers of potatoes as they role-play picking potatoes from a field.

Let's Cook

Smashed Potatoes

- potatoes (12)
- peelers
- knife (for teacher use only)
- 1/4 cup margarine
- 1/2 cup milk
- salt

Invite children to help you wash the potatoes. Peel, cut, and then boil the potatoes in a pot of salted water until tender. Drain. Add 1/4 cup margarine and 1/2 cup milk to the warm potatoes. Encourage children to take turns smashing the potatoes. Add more milk if potatoes are too thick. Serve warm.

Circle Time Themes

Clever Containers

....

As soon as they begin to walk, children love to haul things around. They spend hours filling containers and dumping out the contents. The themes in this section encourage creative play with containers.

....

Pumpkins Round

Let's Look

On a tray, display a medium-sized pumpkin, an orange, and an acorn squash. Cut each in half. Invite children to more closely examine the cut fruit and vegetables. Then place the fruit and vegetables in three separate tubs on a low table. Encourage children to use spoons and cups to collect the seeds from these foods.

Let's Talk

- What is a pumpkin?

- What do you think is inside a pumpkin?

- Where do you think pumpkins grow?

- What can you do with a pumpkin?

- At what special times do you see pumpkins?

Let's Read

Apples and Pumpkins by Anne Rockwell

The Biggest Pumpkin Ever by Steven Kroll

The Magic Pumpkin by Bill Martin, Jr., and John Archambault

Pumpkin Moonshine by Tasha Tudor

The Pumpkin Patch by Elizabeth King

Pumpkin, Pumpkin by Jeanne Titherington

This Year's Garden by Cynthia Rylant

Let's Sing and Say

Did You Ever See a Pumpkin?

(Tune: "Did You Ever See a Lassie?")
Did you ever see a pumpkin,
a pumpkin, a pumpkin?
Did you ever see a pumpkin on the vine?
Did you ever pick a pumpkin,
a pumpkin, a pumpkin?
Did you ever pick a pumpkin from the vine?
Did you ever take a pumpkin home,
pumpkin home, pumpkin home?
Did you ever take a pumpkin home
and cook it for pie?
Did you ever carve a pumpkin,
a pumpkin, a pumpkin?
Did you ever carve a pumpkin
for Halloween night?

Five Little Pumpkins

Five little pumpkins
sitting on a gate,
(Hold up five fingers.)
The first one said,
"Oh, my it's getting late."
(Hold up thumb.)
The second one said,
"There are bats in the air."
(Hold up index finger.)
The third one said,
"I don't care."
(Hold up middle finger.)
The fourth one said,
"Let's run, run, run."
(Hold up ring finger.)
The fifth one said,
"I'm ready for fun."
(Hold up little finger.)
Then wooooo went the wind,
(Wave hands back and forth.)
And out went the light.
(Clap hands loudly.)
Five little pumpkins
rolled out of sight.
(Roll hands one over the other.)

Jack-o'-Lantern

I'm sometimes big,
(Hold arms in a circle overhead.)
I'm sometimes small,
(Form a small circle with hands.)
But always round and yellow.
(Form a medium circle with hands.)
When children fix my famous grin,
(Smile and point to lips.)
Then I'm a scary fellow.
(Make a scary face.)

Pumpkin, Pumpkin

(Tune: "Twinkle, Twinkle, Little Star")
Pumpkin, pumpkin nice and round,
Lying on the cool, soft ground.
Once you were a seed so small.
Now you are a big, round ball.
Pumpkin, pumpkin, nice and round,
Lying on the cool, soft ground.

Let's Move

- **Rocking Pumpkins**

Invite children to sit on the floor crossed-legged, holding their knees and rocking, like round pumpkins.

Let's Make

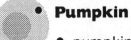

- **Pumpkin Prints**

  - pumpkin rind

  - plastic knives and forks

  - tempera paint (red, yellow, green)

  - styrofoam meat trays

  - grocery bags

Cut a 3" cube of pumpkin rind for each child to use to make pumpkin prints. Invite children to carve designs in the rind using plastic knives and forks. Place tempera paint in styrofoam meat trays. Children can dip their carved pumpkin cubes into the paint and press the cubes on brown grocery bag paper. Hang the finished work to dry.

- **Painting Pumpkin Colors**

  - tempera paint (orange, yellow, red, green)

  - cinnamon, nutmeg, clove, and pumpkin pie spice

  - paintbrushes

  - drawing paper

Mix various amounts of red, yellow, orange, and green paint to produce shades of persimmon, tangerine, tomato, and mustard. Sprinkle cinnamon, nutmeg, cloves, and pumpkin pie spice into the mixed paints for wonderful fall aromas. Encourage children to explore painting designs with the pumpkin colors. Some children may choose to paint pumpkin shapes.

Pumpkin Patch Mat

- brown and green felt
- green rug yarn
- plastic bags
- clay (see recipe for clay #1 on page 268)
- plastic bags
- orange food coloring
- cloves
- glue
- scissors

Cut small leaves from green felt. Give each child a 9" x 12" piece of brown felt, several 9" pieces of rug yarn, and some green felt leaves. Invite children to glue the yarn in rows horizontally across the brown felt. Have children glue the leaves on each side of the yarn to look like pumpkin vines. Then prepare clay according to the directions on page 268 and place the clay in plastic bags. Squeeze a few drops of orange food coloring in each bag and invite children to help knead the clay to mix the color. Remove the clay from the bags and knead until smooth and firm. Invite children to pinch off small amounts of clay and roll it into balls. Children can push a clove into the top of each ball to form a pumpkin stem. Air dry the dough balls in a warm place away from direct sunlight. Place the mats and dried clay pumpkins in the block center. Add dump trucks to encourage harvest play.

Let's Play

• Washing Pumpkin Seeds

Props: pumpkin, tubs of water, slotted spoons, sieves, and a tray lined with paper towels

Cut a pumpkin and scoop out the seeds. Invite children to wash the seeds using water, slotted spoons, and sieves. Place the clean seeds on a tray lined with paper towels. Dry the seeds and save them for roasting or planting.

• The Great Pumpkin Floating Debate

Props: water table; tiny pumpkins, squash, and gourds; plastic pumpkins of various sizes; aquarium nets; sieves; and tongs

Invite children to predict which items will float and which will sink. Encourage children to test their predictions. Invite children to retrieve the vegetables from the water with nets and tongs.

• Pumpkin Detectives

Props: pumpkins (different sizes and density), produce scale, adding machine tape, tape measures, plastic knives, magnifying glasses, toy cameras, stamp pad and paper, construction paper, scissors, tape, caps, glasses with funny noses, and wigs

Encourage children to observe how pumpkins are alike and how they are different as they pretend to be "pumpkin detectives." Read or tell the story of *The Vanishing Pumpkin*. Talk to children about gathering clues and examining the pumpkins you have collected. Demonstrate how to use some of the equipment and some possible identification techniques. Encourage children to weigh and measure pumpkins, scrape samples to examine under a magnifying glass, and create pumpkin disguises using appropriate props.

Let's Cook

Pumpkin Pancakes

- 2 eggs
- 1/4 cup oil
- honey
- 1 1/2 cups milk (lowfat)
- 2 cups flour

- 1/2 tsp salt
- 1/2 tsp pumpkin pie spice
- 1/4 cup wheat germ
- food coloring (yellow and red)
- raisins

In a large bowl, beat the eggs. Stir in the oil, 2 tablespoons honey, and milk. Add the dry ingredients and stir the mixture until most of the lumps are gone. Add a bit of yellow and red food coloring to give the mixture an orange tint. Pour the batter, 1/4 cup at a time, onto a hot griddle or skillet. Turn the pancakes when bubbles appear. Invite children to push raisins into their warm pancakes to make eyes, noses, and mouths. Top with honey.

Brown Baggin'

Let's Look

Prepare a small mystery bag for each child. Place a different object in each bag, such as a feather, plastic comb, rock, pinecone, ball, key, spoon, dried beans, cotton ball, crayon, sponge, or quarter. Invite each child to predict what is inside his or her bag by touching the bag, smelling it, or listening to the sound it makes when shaken. After making a guess, invite children to open their bags to check on the contents.

Let's Talk

- What do you think is in your bag?

- What does it feel like?

- How does it sound?

- How does it smell?

- What else would fit in your bag?

- What kinds of things do you often carry in a bag?

Let's Read

Bag Full of Nothing by Jay Williams

The Little Red Hen by Paul Galdone

Morris' Disappearing Bag by Rosemary Wells

The Night of the Paper Bag Monsters by Helen Craig

What's in Fox's Sack? by Paul Galdone

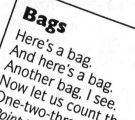

Let's Sing and Say

Bags

Here's a bag.
And here's a bag.
Another bag, I see.
Now let us count them.
One-two-three.
(Point to the pretend bags as you count.)

Five Little Paper Bags

Five little paper bags sitting on the floor—
José took the blue one, and now there are four.
Four little paper bags, as pretty as can be—
Josh took the yellow one, and now there are three.
Three little paper bags and one belongs to you—
You took the purple one, and now there are two.
Two little paper bags, filled with lots of fun—
Lisa took the green one, and now there is one.
One little paper bag all alone you see.
I like it the very best, because it is for me.
(Begin by holding up five fingers, put one down as you count. Point to self when you say "me.")

What's in My Bag?

(Tune: "The Muffin Man")
Do you know what's in my bag,
What's in my bag, what's in my bag?
Do you know what's in my bag?
I'll tell you right now.
(Name what's in your bag.)

The Mask

First you take a big brown bag,
Then you fold it so.
Next you cut two scary eyes,
And a great big nose.
Cut some holes for arms,
And color lines with red.
Add frizzy hair, a big green nose,
And put it over your head. Boo!
(Go through the hand motions of making a mask.)

Let's Move

- ### Beanbags

Play music while children walk around the classroom balancing beanbags on their heads, shoulders, or feet. Challenge children to crawl with the beanbags on their backs or scoot on their backs with the beanbags on their stomachs.

Let's Make

- ### Paper-Bag Monsters

  - grocery bags (one per child)

  - scissors

  - tempera paint

  - paintbrushes

  - collage materials (paper scraps, bottle caps, packing chips, yarn and buttons)

  - glue

Cut eyes and armholes in a large brown grocery bag for each child. Invite children to paint designs on their bags. Children can add collage materials to create noses, mouths, and hair for their bag monsters.

 Brown Bag Puppet Theater

- brown lunch bags (one per child)

- yarn

- buttons

- stickers

- markers

- glue

- large box

Invite children to make paper-bag puppets. Children can glue yarn (5" lengths) and buttons on the bags to make hair and eyes. Invite children to add stickers and use markers to add other details. Children can help decorate a large box to use for a puppet theater. Encourage children to create their own puppet shows.

Let's Play

Sand Bags

Props: sand table, bags, and cups

Encourage children to fill bags with sand. As children play, ask such questions as "How many cups of sand does it take to fill a lunch bag?"

First Time Circle Time

Variety Store

Props: small toys, jewelry, cooking items, sunglasses, pocketbooks, hats, small shopping bags, cash register, child-sized carts, broom and dust pan, price tags and labels, and construction paper

Invite children to create a variety store with the props listed. Children can make "open" and "closed" signs out of construction paper. Encourage children to pretend to shop and take items home in shopping bags.

Bags in Water

Props: water table, assortment of bags (paper, plastic, cloth), and a hole punch

Encourage children to experiment with the bags at the water table to see which ones will float and which ones will hold water. Punch holes in some of the bags.

Let's Cook

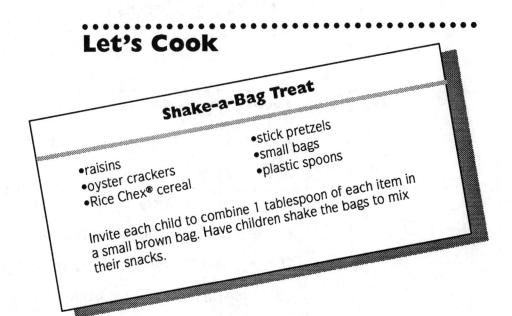

Shake-a-Bag Treat

- raisins
- oyster crackers
- Rice Chex® cereal

- stick pretzels
- small bags
- plastic spoons

Invite each child to combine 1 tablespoon of each item in a small brown bag. Have children shake the bags to mix their snacks.

Bountiful Baskets

Let's Look

Bring a picnic basket to circle time filled with small paper plates and an individual baggie snack for each child. Spread a colorful tablecloth or bed sheet on the floor and invite children to sit around the cloth. Ask children what they think is in the basket. Then take out the plates and baggie snacks and enjoy a snack together.

Let's Talk

- What is a basket?

- What are baskets made of?

- What can you carry in a basket?

- Who carries baskets?

- What else can you use baskets for?

Let's Read

Aunt Nina's Visit by Franz Brandenberg

Basket by George-Ella Lyon

Don't Forget the Bacon by Pat Hutchins

Little Red Riding Hood by Paul Galdone

The Shopping Basket by John Burningham

The Teddy Bear's Picnic by Jimmy Kennedy

Let's Sing and Say

The Sleeping Baby

See the little baby sleeping so sound.
(Cradle arms like holding a baby.)
His (Her) bed is a basket soft and round.
(Rock arms back and forth.)

The Basket Game

(Tune: "Paw-Paw Patch")
Where, oh where are all the children?
Where, oh where are all the children?
Where, oh where are all the children?
Down in the meadow picking daisy crowns.
Picking up daisies, putting them in a basket.
Picking up daisies, putting them in a basket.
Picking up daisies, putting them in a basket.
Way down yonder in the meadow green.

Where, oh where are all the children?
Where, oh where are all the children?
Where, oh where are all the children?
Down in the forest picking acorn caps.

Picking up acorns, putting them in a basket.
Picking up acorns, putting them in a basket.
Picking up acorns, putting them in a basket.
Way down yonder in the forest green.

The Apple Basket

One apple, two apples,
three apples, four,
(Imitate picking apples from a tree.)
Put them in a basket,
Now let's pick some more.
Five apples, six apples,
seven apples, eight,
(Continue picking.)
Hurry up and finish,
it's getting late.

A-Tisket, A-Tasket

A-tisket, a-tasket,
a green and yellow basket.
I wrote a letter to my friend,
and on the way I lost it,
I lost it, I lost it,
and on the way I lost it.
A little boy picked it up
and put it in his pocket.
*(Invite children to stand in a circle
while one child ("it") skips around
the outside of the circle.
The skipping child drops a letter
behind another child. This child
chases "it" around the circle.)*

Let's Move

• A-Tisket, A-Tasket

Invite children to stand in a circle with their hands behind them (palms up) to form a basket. Choose one child to be "it." Give this child an envelope to represent a letter. "It" moves around the outside of the circle and eventually places the letter in one child's hands. "It" tries to run back to his or her place in the circle before being tagged by the child who received the letter. If the new child does not tag "it," he or she becomes the new "it" and the game continues. Other children in the circle can sing "A-Tisket, A-Tasket."

How To Make A Paper Plate Basket

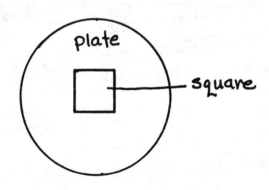

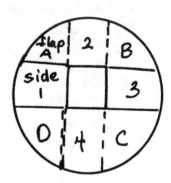

plate

square

① ✏️ ➡ ☐

② Draw — and ⋮

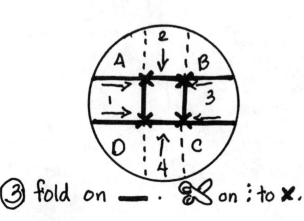

③ fold on — . ✂ on ⋮ to ✗.

④ Staple A and B to 2
and C and D to 4

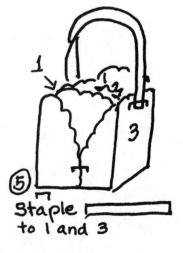

⑤ Staple ▭
to 1 and 3

Let's Make

Paper-Plate Baskets

- paper plates (one per child)
- crayons or markers
- stickers
- cardboard (4" square)
- pencil
- stapler
- construction-paper strips
- shredded paper or plastic grass

Give each child a paper plate to decorate with stickers. Encourage children to add designs using crayons or markers. To transform each plate into a basket, place a 4" cardboard square in the center of each plate and trace around it. Remove the square and extend the vertical sides of the square by drawing dotted lines to the end of the plate. Extend the horizontal sides of the square by drawing solid lines to the edge of the plate. Cut on the dotted lines and fold on the solid lines to form a box with rounded edges. Staple the sides together and add a construction-paper strip for a handle. Children can fill the baskets with shredded paper or plastic grass.

Basket Tubs

- cardboard containers (from products, such as nuts, chips, or oatmeal)
- construction paper
- glue
- watercolors
- paintbrushes
- plastic milk jugs
- scissors

Cover each cardboard container with white or pastel construction paper. Invite children to decorate the containers with watercolor designs. Let the paint dry and then add a plastic handle cut from the side of a plastic milk jug. Children can fill the containers with their favorite things.

Let's Play

Basket of Clothes

Props: basket of old clothes (shirts, socks, pants, skirts, gloves), clothespins, and a clothesline

Stretch a low clothesline across a corner of the room near a wall. Invite children to hang the clothes on the line and secure them with clothespins.

Basket of Fun

Props: baskets, beanbags, and masking tape

Encourage children to take turns tossing beanbags into a basket from different distances. Tape X's on the floor to mark places where children can stand when tossing the bags.

Berry Best Sand and Water Baskets

Props: sand or water table and strawberry or tomato baskets

Invite children to use the baskets to make impressions in wet sand. Encourage children to look for baskets with different designs on the bottom. Children can also use the baskets as sieves using dry sand or water.

Let's Cook

Muffin Baskets

- muffin mix
- paper cupcake liners
- cream cheese (softened)
- chenille stems (1 per child)

Bake your favorite muffins and give one to each child. Invite children to spread cream cheese on top of their muffins. Children can push one end of a chenille stem into the top on each side of the muffins to form basket handles.

Buckets-o'-Fun

Let's Look

Bury an assortment of shells or driftwood in a large bucket of sand. Place the bucket in the center of a plastic drop cloth at circle time. Give each child an opportunity to dig in the sand with a small shovel to find a "treasure." Place all the treasures around the bucket.

Let's Talk

- What are buckets?
- What can buckets hold?
- What can you carry in a bucket?
- Why do we need buckets?

Let's Read

Floating and Sinking by Terry Jennings

Harry by the Sea by Gene Zion

It's Summertime! by Elaine Good

Push Pull Empty Full by Tana Hoban

Sand Cake by Frank Asch

Sunshine by Jan Ormerod

Let's Sing and Say

Did You Ever Fill a Bucket?

(Tune: "Did You Ever See a Lassie?")
Did you ever fill a bucket, a bucket, a bucket?
Did you ever fill a bucket with water like this?
Slosh it this way and that way,
and this way and that way.
Did you ever fill a bucket with water like this?

Did you ever swing a bucket, a bucket, a bucket?
Did you ever swing a bucket around you like this?
Swing this way and that way,
and this way and that way.
Did you ever swing a bucket around you like this?

Five Little Seashells

Five little seashells gone out to sea,
Wait until morning and they'll return to me.
I'll bring my bucket and guess what I'll do?
I'll collect all five and share them with you.

My Red Bucket

(Tune: "Here We Go 'Round the Mulberry Bush")
Oh, do you have a red bucket, a red bucket, a red bucket?
Oh, do you have a red bucket with a handle on top?
Oh, can you fill your bucket, your bucket, your bucket?
Oh, can you fill your bucket with sand up to the top?

Buckets

(Tune: "London Bridge")
I take my bucket to the beach,
to the beach, to the beach.
I take my bucket to the beach
and fill it up with sand.

I take my bucket to the tub,
to the tub, to the tub.
I take my bucket to the tub
and fill it up with water.

(Invite children to create new verses.)

Let's Move

Beach Play

Invite children to pretend they are collecting shells in a bucket. Children can walk around looking carefully for shells and bend down to pick them up. Children can pretend to fill a bucket with sand and then turn it over to make a sand castle.

Let's Make

Plaster of Paris Sand Casts

- seashells

- vaseline

- bucket of wet sand

- plaster of Paris

Invite each child to choose a seashell and coat it with vaseline. Children can press the shells into the wet sand to make impressions. Carefully remove the seashells and fill the impressions with plaster of Paris. Allow the plaster to dry and then remove the hardened plaster shells. These make nice gifts for family members or friends.

Buckets and Balls

- plastic buckets with lids

- construction paper

- scissors

- tempera paint

- two small rubber balls

Cut construction paper to fit around the inside of each bucket. Holding each bucket on its side, drop tempera paint on the paper. Place two small rubber balls in each bucket and secure the lids. Invite each child to hold a bucket and shake it. Then encourage children to open the lids and remove the paper that now will have interesting and colorful prints. Rinse out the buckets and put another sheet of construction paper inside each to make a new design.

Let's Play

Beaches

Props: small wading pool filled with sand, buckets, plastic containers, funnels, and cubes

Keep the sand in the wading pool slightly damp so children can use buckets and plastic containers to mold shapes. Invite children to make sand towers, castles, walls, and so on.

Bucket Game

Props: bucket and clothespins

Encourage children to count how many clothespins they can drop in the bucket.

Sand and Water Fun

Props: sand or water table, various sizes of buckets, and seashells

Invite children to experiment with filling and emptying buckets with sand, water, and seashells.

Let's Cook

Bucket Punch

- fresh berries
- ice cube trays
- raspberry sherbet
- frozen white grape juice concentrate (1 large can)
- clean bucket
- paper cups

Fill ice cube trays with water, place fresh berries in each section, and then freeze. Mix grape juice concentrate with water in a clean bucket and add scoops of sherbet. Add the berry ice cubes and enjoy bucket punch with the children.

Circle Time Themes

Marvelous Make-Believe

With budding imaginations, young children like to explore the realms of fantasy. Through make-believe, children act out fears, search for power, and learn about themselves. The themes in this section introduce fantasy characters in non-threatening ways and encourage children to expand their creativity.

Mild-Mannered Monsters

Let's Look

Hang a sheet in the circle time area and shine a light behind it. Give children hats, paper tubes, and other props and encourage children to experiment creating shadows. Two or more children can join together to create a monster with several legs and arms.

Let's Talk

- What do monsters look like?

- Where do monsters live?

- What kinds of sounds do monsters make?

- Are monsters afraid of anything?

- Are monsters real or make-believe?

- Are you afraid of monsters? Why or why not?

Let's Read

Clyde Monster by Robert L. Crowe

I'm Coming to Get You by Tony Ross

Little Monsters by Jan Pienkowski

My Mama Says There Aren't Any Zombies, Ghosts, Vampires, Creatures, Demons, Monsters, Fiends, Goblins, or Things by Judith Viorst

Some of My Best Friends Are Monsters by Rob Paige

Where the Wild Things Are by Maurice Sendak

Let's Sing and Say

Five Little Monsters

This little monster has a big red nose.
This little monster has purple toes.
This little monster plays all night.
This little monster is such a fright.
And this little monster goes,
"Tee-hee-hee."
"I'm not scary. I'm just silly me."
(Hold up hand and point to each finger.)

If You Are a Monster

(Tune: "If You're Happy and You Know It")
If you're a monster and you know it,
wave your arms.
If you're a monster and you know it,
wave your arms.
If you're a monster and you know it,
your arms will surely show it.
If you're a monster and you know it,
wave your arms.

Invite children to suggest additional verses,
for example:
… show your claws.
… gnash your teeth.
… stomp your feet.

The Monsters Are So Loud

(Tune: "When Johnny Comes Marching Home")
The monsters stomp around the house,
Boom! Boom! Boom! Boom!
The monsters stomp around the house,
Boom! Boom! Boom! Boom!
The monsters stomp around the house,
Their brothers and sisters send them out
And they stomp some more
outside around the house.

The monsters yell around the house,
Eeeeeh! Eeeeeh!
The monsters yell around the house,
Eeeeeh! Eeeeeh!
The monsters yell around the house,
Their brothers and sisters send them out
And they yell some more
outside around the house.

Ten Little Monsters

(Tune: "Ten Little Indians")
One little, two little, three little monsters,
Big wild eyes and skin with fuzzy furs.
Climbing on the stairs
when no one knows they're there.
Heigh-ho, monsters are here.

One little, two little, three little trolls,
Playing in the woods
where fern and moss grow.
Running through the trees
and having lots of fun.
Heigh-ho, monsters are here.

Let's Move

Merry Monsters

Make a monster wand for each child by punching holes in one end of paper-towel cardboard tubes. Tie an assortment of fabric strips in the holes to make colorful fringe. Then invite children to dance like merry monsters while waving the wands. Play slow, floating music. Encourage children to use all the space around them and incorporate slow, gliding movements as well as movements that are short and quick. When the music stops, invite the "monsters" to lie down for a rest.

Let's Make

Monster Puppets

- white paper bags (one per child)
- colored sticker circles
- markers
- yarn
- glue
- newspaper
- cardboard tubes (one per child)
- tape

Invite children to use colored stickers and markers to make monster faces on the side of several paper bags. Children can use yarn to make monster hair. Stuff the bags with newspaper balls and use tape to attach a cardboard tube to each stuffed bag for a handle.

Monster Masks

- stockings and tights (assorted colors)
- wire coat hangers (one per child)
- yarn
- plastic darning needles
- buttons
- paper scraps

- glue
- duct tape or masking tape

Bend wire coat hangers into diamond shapes with the hook twisted together to form a handle. Wrap tape around the handles and make sure there are no sharp ends. Invite children to choose stockings to pull over the wire frames. Secure the stockings at the bottom of the hangers. Then show the children how to stitch yarn to the stockings to make hair and mouths. Children can add buttons and paper scraps to make eyes and noses. The finished masks make wonderful props for monster stories and dances.

Let's Play

Monster Makeup Shop

Props: large T-shirts, football shoulder pads, wigs, headbands with horns, rubber animal noses, large furry slippers, gloves with felt claws glued to the fingertips, rubber ears, and a full-length mirror

Display the props listed on pegs or low shelves. Explain to children that this "monster makeup shop" is only for funny, happy monsters. Give the children enough time to freely explore this center and the unusual props. Be sensitive to children who may be frightened by the costumes.

Monster Make-a-Face

Props: felt face shapes, felt facial features, cotton balls, and yarn

Cut four face-shaped ovals from felt and glue them each to a cardboard square. Then cut four sets of facial features from felt and glue to the smooth side of sandpaper. Cut out these sandpaper-felt shapes and place them in a basket. Add colored cotton balls and pieces of yarn to the basket and invite children to use the facial features, cotton, and yarn to create monster faces on the felt face boards.

Monster Mansions

Props: Spanish moss, small troll dolls or monster figurines, pieces of mesh produce bags, bells, and small twigs anchored in clay bases

Display the props listed above on a cloth spread on the floor. Discuss with children ways they could use the props to create monster mansions. Invite children to try out their ideas by making the classroom into a monster community.

Wild Things Waterworks

Props: *Where the Wild Things Are* by Maurice Sendak, water table, styrofoam island, pencils, leaf-shaped pieces of green felt, small boats, and monster figures

After reading *Where the Wild Things Are*, add the props listed to the water table. Glue green felt leaves to the ends of pencils to make palm trees and stick the palm trees in the styrofoam island. Encourage children to pretend to make Max's journey.

Let's Cook

Monster Mash

- 6 eggs
- 2 cups cottage cheese (lowfat)
- 4 Tbsp oil
- 1/2 cup flour
- 1/4 tsp salt
- paper cups (3-oz size)
- small paper plates
- plastic spoons
- food coloring
- pancake syrup
- raisins

Combine the eggs and cottage cheese in a blender. Add the oil, flour, and salt and blend until smooth. Divide the batter into eight (3-oz) cups. Give each child a cup and invite children to add food coloring to the batter. Help each child pour the batter onto the grill in a monster shape. Cook the batter until bubbles form on the surface. Be sure to cook out of reach of the children. Turn and cook until golden. Place a pancake on each child's plate. Invite children to add raisin mouths, noses, and eyes. Serve with syrup. Serves 8.

Shy Elves and Lovely Fairies

Let's Look

Before children arrive, tape elf feet (made from felt or construction paper) from the classroom doorway to the circle time area. Place a small hat in the center of the circle. Leave other clues that suggest an elf may have visited the classroom, such as tiny shoes, gold coins, and small wire glasses. When children come to circle time, point out the clues and invite children to suggest who may have left these items lying around.

Let's Talk

- Who do you think left the tiny footprints?

- What other clues do you see?

- What is an elf?

- What do elves like to play?

- Where do elves live?

- What is a fairy?

- Where do fairies live?

- Are elves and fairies real or make-believe?

Let's Read

Children of the Forest by Elsa Beskow

Elfabet: An ABC of Elves by Jane Yolen

A Fairy Went-a-Marketing by Rose Fyleman

Mogwogs on the March by Oliver Dunrea

Peter in Blueberry Land by Elsa Beskow

The Wizard, the Fairy, and the Magic Chicken by Helen Lester

The Little Elf

(Tune: "The Farmer in the Dell")
There was a little elf,
Who lived upon a shelf.
He slept all day
And then at night
he tiptoed out to play.

There was a little elf,
Who lived all by himself.
He had a house
down by the creek
But he ran away
if you tried to peek.

Elves and Fairies

(Tune: "When Johnny Comes Marching Home Again")
The elves go tiptoe in the dark,
Hoorah! Hoorah!
The elves go tiptoe in the dark,
Hoorah! Hoorah!
The elves go tiptoe in the dark,
They go so quietly through the park,
That we never hear them tiptoe in the dark.

The fairies go flying through the night,
Hoorah! Hoorah!
The fairies go flying through the night,
Hoorah! Hoorah!
The fairies go flying through the night,
Their wings look lovely in the light,
As they flutter softly through the quiet night.

The elves go dancing on the moon,
Hoorah! Hoorah!
The elves go dancing on the moon.
Hoorah! Hoorah!
The elves go dancing on the moon,
They skip and jump and leap and swoon,
But we've never seen them dancing on the moon.

The Elf

Here is an elf as tiny as can be.
(Hold up two fingers
as if measuring height.)
And here is his home
in a hole in this tree.
(Form a large, round circle with hands.)
When a strange noise he hears
(Make a "whoo-oo" noise.)
He perks up his ears.
And runs to his hole in the tree.

The Fairies

Fairies are so lovely
With silver wings that shine.
(Lock thumbs and spread
hands like wings.)
They flutter
through the meadow
(Flutter hands.)
And light upon the pine.
(Stop.)
They sweep away the cobwebs
And paint the flowers new.
(Imitate these motions.)
They take a bath in buttercups
(Form a buttercup with fingers.)
And wash their hair in dew.
(Touch hair.)

Let's Move

Fairies and Giants

Invite children to creep around like tiny fairies. Then invite children to stomp around loudly like giants. Encourage children to crouch down and be very small and then stand on their tiptoes to be very tall.

Let's Make

Elf Homes

- shoebox lids (one per child)
- nature items (dried moss, leaves, acorns, flowers, dried grasses)
- glue
- paintbrushes

Give each child a shoebox lid. Invite children to use paintbrushes to spread the lids with glue. Then encourage children to arrange an assortment of nature items on the lids to make elf homes.

Magic Elf Hats

- construction paper (12" x 18")
- shiny materials (gummed stars, glitter, mylar strips, ribbons)
- glue
- pom poms
- paintbrushes
- stapler

Give each child a 12" x 18" sheet of construction paper. Invite children to glue some of the "magical" shiny items to the paper to make magic elf hats. When the papers are dry, fold into cone-shaped hats to fit each child's head and carefully staple. Fold down the pointed end and staple on a pom pom.

Fairy Crowns

- metallic bulletin-board trim
- gold and silver doilies
- shredded foil
- sequins
- glue
- stapler

Cut a strip of bulletin-board trim to fit around each child's head. Invite children to glue doilies, foil, and sequins on their crowns. When the strips are dry, staple to form headbands.

Let's Play

● **Elf Houses**

Props: large cardboard box, paint, umbrella, dishes, and hats

Make an elf house for the children. Paint a large cardboard box to look like a tree and cut an opening large enough for a child to crawl through. Place an open umbrella over the top. Then invite children to pretend to be elves as they go in and out of the house. Children can wear elf hats and prepare a pretend meal using the dishes.

Let's Cook

Elf Muffins

- bran muffin mix
- miniature muffin baking cups
- small paper plates

Make bran muffins following the package directions. Bake in tiny muffin tins and serve on tiny paper plates.

Silly Clowns

Let's Look

Set up a flannelboard in the circle time area. Include felt eyes, noses, mouths, and hair. Invite children to take turns making clown faces on the flannelboard. Or, appear in the circle wearing a clown costume. If you choose to paint your face, use only minimal amounts of makeup. Keep in mind that some children may be frightened by painted faces.

Let's Talk

- What is a clown?

- Have you ever seen a clown? Where?

- How do clowns act?

- Can you make a happy, sad, or silly clown face?

- What do clowns wear?

Let's Read

Circus! by Jack Prelutsky

The Circus by Brian Wildsmith

Clown by Paul Manning

The Clown-Arounds by Joanna Cole

If I Ran the Circus by Dr. Seuss

The Little Engine That Could by Wally Piper

Up and Down on the Merry-Go-Round by Bill Martin, Jr., and John Archambault

Let's Sing and Say

Putting on a Clown Face

(Tune: "Lazy Mary, Will You Get Up")
First you paint your face orange,
Your face orange,
Your face orange.
(Rub face.)
Oh, first you paint your face orange,
And pat it like this.
(Pat face.)

Next you put on eyebrows,
On eyebrows,
On eyebrows.
(Pretend to draw on eyebrows.)
Next you put on eyebrows,
And pat them like this.
(Pat eyebrows.)

Now, you draw a big mouth,
A big mouth,
A big mouth.
(Pretend to draw a mouth.)
Now, you draw a big mouth,
And color it in.
(Pretend to color inside outline.)

Next you draw some round cheeks,
Some round cheeks,
Some round cheeks.
(Rub cheeks in circular motion.)
Oh, next you draw some round cheeks,
And pat them like this.
(Pat cheeks.)

Last you put on a big nose,
A big nose,
A big nose.
(Pretend to put on a nose.)
Oh, last you put on a big nose,
And now you are done!
(Pat nose and wave.)

Mr. Clown, Silly Fellow

(Tune: "Punchinella")
*(One child stands in the center
of the circle as "Mr. Clown."
The other children walk around
him or her while singing.)*
What can you do,
Mr. Clown, silly fellow?
What can you do,
Mr. Clown, silly you?
*(Invite child to imitate a clown action,
such as jumping or walking.
Children then imitate his or her action.)*
We can do it, too,
Mr. Clown, silly fellow.
We can do it, too,
Mr. Clown, silly you.

Silly Clown

(Tune: "Old MacDonald Had a Farm")
I'm a silly little clown,
see what I can do.
I can make a silly face.
Can you make one, too?
See my silly, silly mouth
and my silly, silly nose.
See my mouth and my nose.
I'm silly, silly all the time.
I'm a silly little clown,
see what I can do.
*(Repeat, substituting "sad," "angry,"
or "frightened" in place of "silly.")*

The Clowns

Here come the clowns
Marching up and down.
(Walk fingers across the air.)
One has on a yellow hat
(Form a hat with hands.)
One is holding a silly bat.
(Pretend to swing a bat.)
One is wearing an orange wig.
(Pat pretend hair.)
One has pants that are too big.
(Hold up pants.)
Here come the clowns
Marching up and down.
(Walk fingers across the air.)
'Round and 'round
and 'round the town,
Marching up and down.
(Roll hands and "march" fingers.)

Five Little Clowns

Five little clowns on the circus floor—
(Hold up five fingers.)
One did a somersault, then there were four.
Four little clowns standing on one knee—
(Hold up four fingers.)
One fell over backwards, then there were three.
Three little clowns with hair of red and blue—
(Hold up three fingers.)
One rode on an elephant, then there were two.
Two little clowns having so much fun—
(Hold up two fingers.)
One flew on the trapeze, then there was one.
One little clown in the ring all alone—
(Hold up one finger.)
He stood on a tiger and ate an ice-cream cone.

Five Funny Clowns

One funny clown,
(Hold up one finger.)
Begins to sneeze.
(Hold finger under nose.)
Two funny clowns,
(Hold up two fingers.)
Fall on their knees.
*(Hold hands up, palms facing,
then drop hands down.)*
Three funny clowns,
(Hold up three fingers.)
Wear floppy shoes.
(Hold hands out, palms down.)
Four funny clowns,
(Hold up four fingers.)
Read the news.
(Hold a pretend paper.)
Five funny clowns,
(Hold up five fingers.)
Take a bow.
(Bow head.)
The circus act is over now
That's all!
(Hold hands up.)

Let's Move

Clowning Around

Invite children to create silly clown acts that include funny facial expressions and silly movements.

Let's Make

Clown Flags

- white cotton or muslin fabric
- scissors
- cardboard tubes
- glue
- markers

Cut fabric into triangles, squares, and rectangles. Make sure that one side of each shape is at least 6" long. Then invite children to choose a fabric shape and decorate it using markers. Help children glue the 6" side of their flags around cardboard tubes to make handles for the flags.

Shakers

- styrofoam plates
- aquarium gravel or tiny pebbles
- stapler
- masking tape
- collage materials (ribbon, shiny star stickers, bits of foil, streamers)
- glue

Place a small amount of aquarium gravel or pebbles between two paper plates. Put masking tape around the plate edges and secure with staples. Make one shaker for each child to decorate with collage materials.

Clown Horns

- cardboard tubes

- glue

- collage materials (ribbon, shiny star stickers, bits of foil, streamers)

- crayons or markers

- waxed paper

- rubberbands

Invite each child to decorate a cardboard tube using collage materials and crayons or markers. Help children secure a small piece of waxed paper over one end of each tube with a rubberband. Encourage children to blow and hum through the open ends of the tubes to play their cardboard horns.

Let's Play

Clown Alley

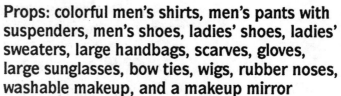

Props: colorful men's shirts, men's pants with suspenders, men's shoes, ladies' shoes, ladies' sweaters, large handbags, scarves, gloves, large sunglasses, bow ties, wigs, rubber noses, washable makeup, and a makeup mirror

Set up a clown's dressing room near the housekeeping center. Invite children to help you collect items for this center. Discuss ways to apply makeup and take care of the costumes. Designate a place to store items with appropriate labels. Provide children with plenty of time to explore this center and its materials.

Block Circus

Props: small hoops, rubber circus animals, large wooden train, bendable rubber clown dolls, small wooden or plastic people, popsicle sticks, clay, and construction paper

Place the props in a box in the block center. Discuss the props with the children and help them discover ways to use them to create a circus atmosphere. For example, children can make signs from construction paper, glue them to popsicle sticks, and secure them in a clay base. Children could also create circus parades with the props, if they wish. Encourage children to use their imaginations.

Backyard Circus

Props: costumes, masking tape, rope, dowels, cardboard tubes, and construction paper

Invite children to plan a classroom circus. Encourage each child to choose an act he or she would like to perform or a role he or she would like to play. Children can be performers, announcers, animals, concession workers, audience members, roustabouts, or ticket salespersons. Help children create props, or invite children to bring costumes and materials from home. Assist children as they plan and implement their circus ideas. Invite family and friends to attend the big event.

Let's Cook

Silly Clown Sandwiches

- English muffins
  (1/2 per child)
- provolone cheese
  (1 round slice per child)
- pepperoni
- olive slices
- pimento slices
- mushroom slices

Toast each muffin half. Invite children to place cheese over their toasted muffins and add small pieces of pepperoni, olives, pimento, and mushrooms on top of the cheese to make silly clown faces. Toast the sandwiches again until the cheese melts. Cool and enjoy.

Magical Moon People

Let's Look

Bring a round mirror to circle time and sit so sunlight is reflected off the mirror onto the wall to resemble a moon. Then invite children to "find the moon." If your classroom does not have windows or it is not a sunny day, use a flashlight to cast a moon shadow on the wall. Invite children to "catch the moon."

Let's Talk

- What is a moon?
- When do you see the moon?
- Where can you see the moon?
- What is the real moon like?
- Do you think there really is a "man in the moon"?

Let's Read

The Moon Is Following Me by Philip Heckman

Moon Man by Tom Ungerer

Moonlight by Jan Ormerod

Papa, Please Get the Moon for Me by Eric Carle

Tom and Pippo See the Moon by Helen Oxenbury

The Turtle and the Moon by Charles Turner

Wait 'til the Moon Is Full by Margaret Wise Brown

Wynken, Blynken and Nod by Eugene Field

Let's Sing and Say

The Moon

I run to my window
to see the moon.
I open the shutters
and let in the night.
(Open pretend shutters.)
I watch the moon
slowly fill up my room,
While little stars dance
in the moonlight.
(Open and shut hands.)

Aiken Drum

Chorus:
There was a man
lived in the moon,
in the moon,
in the moon.
There was a man
lived in the moon,
And his name
was Aiken Drum.
And he played
upon a ladle,
A ladle, a ladle.
And he played
upon a ladle,
And his name
was Aiken Drum.

His hair was made
of green cheese,
of green cheese,
of green cheese.
His hair was made
of green cheese,
And his name
was Aiken Drum.
(Repeat chorus.)

Additional Verses:
His eyes were made
of meatballs...
His coat was made
of pizza ....
His shoes were made
of peanuts...
His pants were made of...
His hat was made of...
*(Invite children to make up
new verses. Repeat
the chorus after each verse.)*

Hey Diddle, Diddle

Hey diddle diddle,
the cat and the fiddle,
The cow jumped
over the moon.
The little dog laughed
to see such a sport,
And the dish ran away
with the spoon.

Let's Move

• Moon Chasers

Darken the room and invite children to move around with "moonlights" (flashlights). Play some appropriate music, such as "Moonlight Sonata."

Let's Make

• Meteor Streamers

- crepe paper
- aluminum foil

Invite each child to make a small aluminum-foil ball. Have children stick the ends of crepe-paper streamers into the foil ball to make "shooting stars." Children can toss the foil balls and watch the streamers trail.

• Moon Masks

- large paper plates
- scissors
- aluminum foil
- glue
- shiny materials (glitter, ribbons, sparkly paper, gummed stars)
- chopsticks or dowels (one per child)
- tape

Cut large paper plates into crescent shapes and cover with aluminum foil. Give one silver crescent to each child. Invite children to add gummed stars, glitter, torn paper, and ribbons to their crescent moons. Tape a chopstick or dowel to the back of each sparkly moon. Tie ribbons to the chopstick or dowel. Cut eye openings so children can see while holding their moon masks in front of their faces.

Nighttime Pictures

- tempera paint (black)

- drawing paper

- salt shaker

- collage materials (shiny star confetti, cotton balls, silver paper)

Invite children to paint a black background on a sheet of drawing paper. While the paint is still wet, children can attach collage materials to make a moon, stars, or clouds. Encourage children to sprinkle salt over the wet paint to make hundreds of tiny stars, too.

Space Vehicles

- paper plates

- toothpicks

- mini-marshmallows

- chickpeas

Soak the chickpeas in water overnight. Invite children to create space vehicles using toothpicks, marshmallows, and chickpeas. Display the vehicles on paper plates.

Let's Play

Going to the Moon

Props: cardboard boxes, tape, and star stickers

Make a spaceship out of cardboard boxes. Cut a door large enough for children to squeeze through. Cut window openings and attach star stickers to the boxes. Then invite children to take turns sitting in the "moonship" and traveling through imaginary space.

Let's Cook

Crescent Moon Pies

- refrigerator biscuits (one per child)
- foil
- butter
- cinnamon and sugar mixture
- apple pie filling
- forks

Preheat oven to 425° F. Give each child a buttered piece of foil. Invite each child to flatten a biscuit into a 4" circle on the foil. Encourage children to sprinkle the biscuits with the cinnamon and sugar mixture. Have children place 1 teaspoon of apple pie filling in the middle of each biscuit. Fold the biscuits over to form half circles. Crimp the edges together with a fork and prick the tops. Place each turnover (on its foil sheet) on a cookie sheet and bake for 20-25 minutes until nicely browned. Remove and cool.

First Time Circle Time

Circle Time Themes

Locomotion Notions

Young children are in constant motion. They love to observe and talk about things that move. The themes in this section provide opportunities for children to experiment with movement and motion.

Bouncy Buses

Let's Look

Bring a toy bus and small figurine-type people to circle time. Model boarding and exiting a bus using the props.

Let's Talk

- What do buses carry?

- Where do buses go?

- Who drives the bus?

- What does the bus driver wear?

- How does the driver know when someone wants to get off the bus?

- Have you ever ridden on a bus? Where did you go?

- What rules should you remember when you ride a bus?

Let's Read

The Bus Stop by Nancy Hellen

Bus Stop Bop by Robin Kingsland

Oh Lewis by Eve Rice

The School Bus by Donald Crews

Wheels by Byron Barton

Wheels by Shirley Hughes

Wheels on the Bus by Paul O. Zelinsky

The Bus Song

The wheels on the bus
go 'round and 'round,
*(Roll hands 'round and
'round over each other.)*
'Round and 'round,
'Round and 'round.
The wheels on the bus
go 'round and 'round
All through the town.

The horn on the bus
goes beep, beep, beep,
(Pretend to beep a horn.)
Beep, beep, beep,
Beep, beep, beep.
The horn on the bus
goes beep, beep, beep
All through the town.

The wipers on the bus
go swish, swish, swish,
*(Swish with forearms
back and forth.)*
Swish, swish, swish,
Swish, swish, swish.
The wipers on the bus
go swish, swish, swish
All through the town.

The people on the bus
go up and down,
(Stand up and sit back down.)
Up and down,
Up and down.
The people on the bus
go up and down
All through the town.

Let's Sing and Say

The School Bus Comes for Me

(Tune: "The Farmer in the Dell")
The school bus comes for me,
The school bus comes for me.
Hey ho, it's time to go,
The school bus comes for me.

First we pick up John,
First we pick up John.
Hey ho, it's time to go,
First we pick up John.

Additional Verses:
Next we pick up…
Then we pick up…
Last we pick up…
(Name all the children.)

Final Verse:
Now we are at school,
Now we are at school.
Clap and cheer,
we're finally here,
Now we are at school.

Here We Go Riding on the Bus

Here we go riding on the bus,
On the bus, on the bus.
Here we go riding on the bus.
We're going to town.

Bus Ride

The big door opens.
(Move hand from side to side.)
Step up and sit down.
*(Stand, making stepping motion,
and then pretend to sit.)*
The driver starts the engine.
(Imitate turning a key.)
And the big bus goes to town.

Let's Move

Bus Passengers

Prepare a bus driver's hat or headband, a rubber or cardboard steering wheel, two round "wheels" (attach round discs to long cardboard tubes), and a cardboard bus stop sign. Choose a child to wear the bus driver hat and carry the steering wheel. Choose two children to carry the wheels and one child to hold up the sign. Invite the "bus driver" to pretend to drive "passengers" around town as the class sings "The Wheels on the Bus" while marching. When the child holds up the stop sign, have the bus driver stop and encourage passengers to get off and on the bus.

Let's Make

• Wheel Prints

- wheel toys (buses, cars, trucks)
- construction paper (12" x 18")
- tempera paint
- styrofoam meat trays

Give each child a 12" x 18" sheet of construction paper and invite children to choose a bus, car, or truck. Put tempera paint in styrofoam meat trays and help children dip their vehicle's wheels in the paint. Invite children to roll the vehicle across construction paper to make terrific designs.

• Roller Art

- butcher paper
- tape
- sponge rollers
- rubberbands
- tempera paint
- shallow trays
- drawing paper

Cover a table with butcher paper and tape the paper in place. Criss-cross rubberbands over sponge rollers. Invite children to roll the sponge rollers in trays of tempera paint and then across drawing paper to make line designs.

Let's Play

• I Am a Bus

Props: large cardboard box, crayons or markers, paper plates, paper bowls, heavy twine, and glue

Decorate the outside of a large cardboard box with the top cut off to look like a bus. Glue paper plates on the sides for wheels and use paper bowls to make headlights and a steering wheel. Attach heavy twine to the "bus" to act like suspenders. Then invite each child to wear the "bus." The child can move his or her feet to propel the vehicle.

• Bus Ride

Props: large appliance box, scissors, chairs, frisbee, tickets, plastic coins, and a bandaid box

Cut four or five bus windows out of a large appliance box. The windows should be at an appropriate height so a child can see out while sitting on a chair. Put two rows of chairs inside the "bus" for passengers. Place a steering wheel (frisbee) in the front. Have tickets, plastic coins, and a money box (bandaid box) available for passengers to use as they board the bus. Encourage children to take turns role-playing being the driver or passengers.

• Road and Buses

Props: toy bus, variety of "road surfaces" (sand, carpet, linoleum), and inclines

Invite children to "drive" a toy bus across a variety of surfaces, such as sand, carpet, and linoleum. Encourage children to notice which surface allows the bus to move most easily. Create hills and valleys with carpet-covered inclines so children can observe how moving uphill and downhill affects speed.

Let's Cook

Busy Bus Biscuit Wheels

- refrigerator biscuits (one per child)
- American cheese (1 slice per child)

Invite children to flatten biscuits with their hands and then place a round cheese slice on their biscuits. Bake according to the directions on the biscuit packaging. When safely cooled, encourage children to eat their biscuit wheels.

Sleek Sleighs

Let's Look

Pack a suitcase with mittens, a hat, a scarf, jingle bells, and a blanket. Tell children that you are going on an adventure and you have everything you need in your suitcase. Open the suitcase and invite children to examine the contents. Encourage children to predict what type of adventure you might be taking.

Let's Talk

- What makes a sleigh move?
- What makes a sled move?
- What would you wear on a sleigh ride?
- Who rides in sleighs?
- What time of year do people use sleighs? Why?

Let's Read

Anna's Red Sled by Patricia Quinlan

First Snow by Emily Arnold McCully

The First Snowfall by Anne and Harlow Rockwell

The Jacket I Wear in the Snow by Shirley Neitzel

Over the River and Through the Woods by Lydia Maria Child

The Snowy Day by Ezra Jack Keats

Stopping by Woods on a Snowy Evening by Robert Frost

Let's Sing and Say

Jingle Bells

Chorus:
Jingle bells, jingle bells,
Jingle all the way.
Oh, what fun it is to ride
In a one-horse open sleigh—
hey!

Jingle bells, jingle bells,
Jingle all the way.
Oh, what fun it is to ride
In a one-horse open sleigh.

Verses:
Dashing through the snow
In a one-horse open sleigh,
O'er the hills we go
Laughing all the way.
Ho, Ho, Ho!

Bells on bobtails ring
Making spirits bright.
What fun it is to ride and sing
A sleighing song tonight.
O…
(Repeat chorus.)

Getting Ready for a Sleigh Ride

Put on your funny cap.
(Form a hat with fingers.)
Now wrap around your shawl.
(Toss a pretend shawl over shoulder.)
Put the blanket in your lap.
(Pull a pretend blanket over knees.)
The snow's begun to fall.
(Flutter hands down like snowflakes.)

Here's a Hill

Here's a hill,
(Hold out bent arm.)
All covered with snow.
(Rub hand over arm.)
And here is the sled,
All ready to go.
(Put the fist of other hand on arm.)
Climb aboard
and hold on tight.
(Imitate holding reins.)
As we slide
through the snow.
On a wintery night.
(Slide fist down arm.)

Let's Move

- **Sleigh Ride**

Play a recording of appropriate music, such as "The Sleigh Ride." Invite children to pretend to be horses and sleigh riders as they move around the room. Provide several cardboard boxes with rope or cloth handles attached to the front. Children can take turns sitting in and pulling the pretend sleighs. Add jingle bells for a special effect.

Let's Make

Teddy Bear Sleighs

- shoeboxes (one per child)
- construction paper
- scissors
- wooden spools
- tempera paint in shallow pans
- glue
- hole punch
- sturdy cord

Give each child a construction-paper strip to exactly fit around the outside of a shoebox. Invite each child to dip the end of a wooden spool in tempera paint and make spool prints on the paper strip. When the paint is dry, help children glue the paper strips around the shoeboxes. Punch a hole in one end of each box and thread sturdy cord through the hole. Knot the end of the cord so children can pull their box sleighs. Encourage children to bring toy bears or other animals from home to ride in their sleighs.

Snowscapes

- white tempera paint
- blue construction paper
- white collage materials (tissue paper, cotton balls, doilies, crepe paper, facial tissue)

Invite children to spread white paint on a sheet of blue paper to make a snowscape. Encourage children to add white collage materials to the wet paintings to make a snow collage.

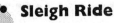

Let's Play

• Sleigh Ride

Props: large cardboard sleigh cut from a refrigerator box, white sheet, cotton balls, chairs, warm blanket or quilt, rope, jingle bells, coats, mittens, scarves, hats, mugs, and an empty cocoa box

Invite children to examine the props and discuss ways to create a sleigh. Place a white sheet under the box sleigh and add cotton balls for snow. If needed, prepare a "sign-up" sheet for children to use to take turns "riding." Encourage children to sign their own names. Then encourage children to role-play going for a sleigh ride. Riders can sit in chairs placed inside the box, place a warm blanket over their laps, and hold the rope reins.

• Winter Wonderland

Props: water table, crushed ice, wool gloves, plastic aprons, small scoops, tubs, blocks of ice, popsicle sticks, toy ships and boats, and white packing material

Fill the water table with crushed ice. Make sure children wear plastic aprons and gloves when playing with ice. Children can use crushed ice to make glaciers, snowpeople, and so on. Add white packing material to the table for snow play on another day.

Let's Cook

Sleigh-Ride Snack

- wheat bread (1 slice per child)
- star, sleigh, or bell cookie cutters
- margarine (softened)
- brown sugar
- small paper cups
- plastic spoons and knives
- sandwich bags

Invite children to cut the bread into shapes using cookie cutters. Have each child mix 1 tablespoon of margarine with 1/2 teaspoon brown sugar in a small paper cup. Then encourage children to spread the mixture on their bread shapes. Toast the bread shapes under a broiler until the tops are brown. Cool the shapes and then place in sandwich bags for sleigh-ride treats.

Amazing Airplanes

Let's Look

Fill a shoebox with a small wooden glider, paper airplane, parachute, and paper helicopter. During circle time, take each item out of the box. Invite children to comment on their observations.

Let's Talk

- What flies in the sky?

- Have you ever seen an airplane?

- Have you ever ridden in an airplane?

- What is an airplane?

- How do airplanes fly?

- What else can fly?

Let's Read

Airport by Byron Barton

The Airport by Gail Gibbons

Angela's Airplane by Robert Munsch

Bored-Nothing to Do by Peter Spier

First Flight by David McPhail

Flying by Don Crews

Planes by Anne Rockwell

Airplane

I am a big airplane,
With wings so wide and strong.
(Hold arms out like wings.)
My tail stands straight up in the air,
And my body's very long.
(Stand on one foot, stretching one leg behind, extended in the air.)
Watch me when I'm flying,
For I go very fast.
(Standing on foot, move extended arms in a flying motion.)
Let's see who can stay up in the air,
And who runs out of gas!
(Encourage children to remain balanced on one foot.)

Three Planes

A little plane.
(Point to an imaginary plane.)
A bigger plane,
(Point again.)
The biggest plane, I see
(Point again.)
Now help me count them.
One, two, three.
(Point on each number.)

My Glider

(Tune: "My Bonnie")
My glider flies over the ocean.
My glider flies over the sea.
My glider flies over the ocean.
Oh, bring back my glider to me.
Bring back, bring back,
Oh, bring back my glider to me, to me.
Bring back, bring back,
Oh, bring back my glider to me.

Fly Away

(Tune: "Mary Had a Little Lamb")
Merrily we fly away, fly away, fly away.
Merrily we fly away, o'er the deep blue sea.
(With arms outstretched like wings, move around the circle while singing.)
Merrily we fly along, fly along, fly along.
Merrily we fly along, o'er the deep blue sea.
(Soar with outstretched arms.)
Merrily we land our plane,
land our plane, land our plane.
Merrily we land our plane
and all go home to rest.
(Sit on the floor and put head in hands.)

Two Little Airplanes

Two little airplanes
sitting on the ground.
(Hold up two hands.)
One was green and
the other was brown.
*(Point with one finger
to right hand and
with another to left hand.)*
Fly away green plane,
(Place left hand behind back.)
Fly away brown.
(Place right hand behind back.)
Come back green plane,
(Bring left hand from back.)
Come back brown.
(Bring right hand from back.)
*(Repeat, saying "four little airplanes."
Hold up four fingers—
two on left hand and two on right.)*

Airplane Ride

I go up, up, up,
(Move hand up like a plane.)
Into the sky.
My wings tip left and right.
(Put fingers out for wings.)
I come down, down, down,
To the ground.
*(Move hand down like
an airplane landing.)*
It was a wonderful flight.

Let's Move

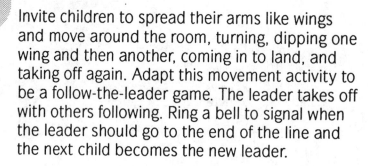

● Airplanes

Invite children to spread their arms like wings
and move around the room, turning, dipping one
wing and then another, coming in to land, and
taking off again. Adapt this movement activity to
be a follow-the-leader game. The leader takes off
with others following. Ring a bell to signal when
the leader should go to the end of the line and
the next child becomes the new leader.

Let's Make

Wing Things

- cardboard

- scissors

- clothespins

- markers

- colored tape

- gummed stars

Cut cardboard into small 3" x 6" rectangles. Give each child a cardboard rectangle and invite children to decorate the rectangles with colored tape and gummed stars to make airplane wings. Children can add other details using markers. Have children clip a wooden clothespin for a "fuselage" to the center of each of the wings.

Sky Mural

- blue butcher paper

- white tempera paint

- cotton balls

- clothespins

Invite children to use cotton balls to paint white clouds on blue butcher paper. Attach the cotton balls to clothespins to help keep the children's fingers clean. Children can also stick cotton balls on the wet paint to add a textured effect.

Let's Play

Pilots

Props: assorted pieces of cardboard, including a large appliance cardboard box, chairs, jar lids, markers, construction paper, serving trays, caps, suitcases, tickets, play food, pillows, magazines, and clipboards

Cut a large appliance box in the shape of an airplane. Attach cardboard wings and place chairs in rows on either side. Invite children to help you make an instrument panel in the cockpit using jar lids and markers. Children can draw arrows and numbers around the jar lids for gauges, as well as "No Smoking" and "Fasten Your Seatbelt" signs. Make a cardboard arch to represent a metal detector at the airport. Encourage children to role-play ticket agents holding clipboards, and so on.

Airport

Props: masking tape, toy airplanes and helicopters, cardboard boxes, flags, windsocks, trucks, and a toy fire truck

Discuss with children props they would need to make an airport. Help children gather necessary materials and construct their ideas. Use masking tape to outline runways on the carpet or floor. Encourage children to "fly" the planes and helicopters into and out of the airport. Children can build hangers for the planes using cardboard boxes.

Let's Cook

Clouds

- Jello
- sliced fruit
- whipped topping
- clear plastic cups
- plastic spoons

Prepare Jello according to the package directions. When set, beat the Jello with a mixer and then layer with fresh fruit and whipped topping in clear plastic cups.

Bobbing Boats

Let's Look

Place a clear tub of water along with a block of wood, styrofoam meat tray, square of aluminum foil, rock, and ball of plasticine clay near the circle time area. Invite children to predict which items will float and which items will sink. Then test the children's predictions. Display pictures of different kinds of boats (rowboats, sailboats, motor boats).

Let's Talk

- What can you ride on in the water?

- How do boats float?

- Have you ever seen a boat?

- Which kinds of boats have you seen?

- Have you ever ridden in a boat?

- Which boats move fast and which ones move more slowly?

Let's Read

Boat Book by Gail Gibbons

Boats by Anne Rockwell

Boats by Byron Barton

Boats by Harriet Ziefert

Boats, Boats, Boats by J. Ruane

Joseph and Nellie by Bijou Le Tord

The Magic Boat by Demi

Mr. Gumpy's Outing by John Burningham

Our Home Is the Sea by Riki Levinson

Who Sank the Boat? by Pamela Allen

Merrily We Sail Along

Merrily we sail along, sail along, sail along.
Merrily we sail along, o'er the deep blue sea.

Michael, Row the Boat Ashore

Michael, row the boat ashore, Hallelujah!
Michael, row the boat ashore, Hallelujah!
Sister, help to trim the sails, Hallelujah!
Sister, help to trim the sails, Hallelujah!
The river is deep and the river is wide, Hallelujah!
Milk and honey on the other side, Hallelujah!

Row, Row, Row Your Boat

Row, row, row your boat,
Gently down the stream.
Merrily, merrily, merrily, merrily
Life is but a dream.
(Divide children into two groups
and sing as a round.)

Boats

Some boats are very big.
(Hold hands far apart.)
Some are very small.
(Hold hands close together.)
Some boats have a tall, tall rig.
(Spread arms vertically.)
Some have none at all.
(Hold palms up to indicate
a flat-bottomed boat.)

Rub-a-Dub-Dub

Rub-a-dub-dub, three men in a tub,
And who do you think they be?
The butcher, the baker,
the candlestick maker,
Turn them out, knaves all three!

Let's Move

Rowing Along

Divide the class into pairs and invite each pair of children to face each other with their feet touching. Children can hold hands and move backward and forward in a rowing motion while singing "Row, Row, Row Your Boat."

Let's Make

Floaters

- styrofoam meat trays
- plastic fast-food containers
- egg cartons
- pipe cleaners
- colored tape
- stickers
- permanent markers
- water tub

Invite children to choose a meat tray, fast-food container, or egg-carton section to make a floater. Encourage children to decorate their floaters using pipe cleaners, colored tape, stickers, and permanent markers. Children can launch their completed crafts in a tub of water to test their floating ability.

Blow Pictures

- tempera paint
- drawing paper
- drinking straws

Help children drip tempera paint onto a large sheet of paper. Give each child half a drinking straw. Invite children to aim the straw at a paint drop and carefully blow through it. The paint will scatter and make colorful designs on the paper.

Let's Play

• Wynken, Blynken, and Nod

Props: large cardboard carton, sheet, empty fabric roll, fishing net, plastic lids, glue, glitter, paper clips, and magnets

Trim the sides of a large cardboard carton to make a shallow box. Attach a piece of sheet to an empty fabric roll. Stand this homemade mast and sail inside the shallow box. Attach a fishing net to one side of the vessel. Cut fish and starfish out of plastic lids. Children can glue glitter to the fish and place a paper clip on the end of each one. Tie or stick magnets to the net. Invite children to drop fish onto the net. The magnets will attract the paper clips attached to the fish and cause some to be caught in the net. Children can remove the fish and cast again.

• Casting for Stars

Props: water table, star sequins, small aquarium nets, strainers, and toy boats

Fill the water table three-quarters full of water and scatter star sequins and boats. Invite children to fish for the stars by catching them in aquarium nets and strainers.

Let's Cook

Sailboats

- hard-boiled eggs (1/2 for each child)
- American cheese (1 slice per child)
- toothpicks
- small paper plates
- knife (for teacher use only)

Peel eggs and then cut them in half. Give each child 1/2 an egg and one slice of American cheese. Help children cut the cheese slices into two rectangular pieces. Children can eat one piece and use a toothpick to attach the other piece to the egg to make a sail.

Circle Time Themes
Terrific Toys

While hundreds of toys enter the market each year, some of the most enjoyable and beneficial are those traditional favorites from the past. The themes in this section are designed to build on these terrific toys.

Building Blocks

Let's Look

Pass around a basket of small wooden blocks and invite each child to take a few. Encourage children to stack their blocks. Then invite children to combine their stacks to make line structures.

Let's Talk

- What can you build with blocks?

- How could you make a train or a tower?

- What else could you use to build a train or tower?

- What else could you make with blocks?

Let's Read

Block Book by Susan A. Couture

Block City by Robert Louis Stevenson

Building a House by Byron Barton

Changes, Changes by Pat Hutchins

Push Pull Empty Full by Tana Hoban

Will I Have a Friend? by Miriam Cohen

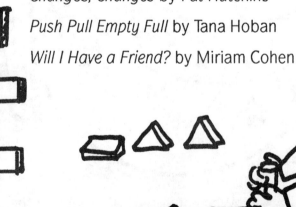

Let's Sing and Say

Build, Build, Build

(Tune: "Row, Row, Row Your Boat")
Build, build, build with blocks,
Towers, roads, and more.
Isn't it such merry fun,
Building on the floor.

Build, build, build a road,
Make it long and straight,
Now let's make a block bridge here,
And then we'll add a gate.

Building with Blocks

(Tune: "Here We Go 'Round the Mulberry Bush")
This is the way we build with blocks,
Build with blocks, build with blocks,
This is the way we build with blocks,
So early in the morning.

This is the way we build up high,
(Imitate building a tower.)
Build up high, build up high,
This is the way we build up high,
So early in the morning.

Johnny Pounds with One Hammer

Johnny pounds with one hammer, one hammer, one hammer.
Johnny pounds with one hammer, then he pounds with two.
Johnny pounds with two hammers, two hammers, two hammers.
Johnny pounds with two hammers, then he pounds with three.
Johnny pounds with three hammers, three hammers, three hammers.
Johnny pounds with three hammers, then he pounds with four.
Johnny pounds with four hammers, four hammers, four hammers.
Johnny pounds with four hammers, then he pounds with five.
Johnny pounds with five hammers, five hammers, five hammers.
Johnny pounds with five hammers, then he goes to sleep.
(Imitate pounding. In the last verse, imitate sleeping.)

The Tower

I place a large block on the floor.
(Imitate placing a block.)
Next I add just one more.
(Again.)
Now, I add a third one.
(Again.)
Building towers is such fun.
I try to place one more on top.
(Imitate placing a block.)
Now, I think I'd better stop.

Let's Move

- **Block Mazes**

  Encourage children to build mazes using cardboard block bricks, shoeboxes, and long unit blocks. Invite children to move through the mazes they have created.

Let's Make

Wood Scrap Sculptures

- wood scraps

- glue

- paper plates

- paintbrushes

- markers or tempera paint

Invite children to make a sculpture by gluing wood scraps to a sturdy paper plate base. Children can decorate their designs with markers or tempera paint.

Block Villages

- boxes (shoeboxes, milk cartons, medicine boxes)

- glue

- cardboard

Invite children to glue boxes on a large cardboard base to make a city or village.

Let's Play

Block Towers

Props: blocks, masking tape, wooden people and zoo animals, and toy vehicles

Encourage children to make block trains and towers in the block center. Before children arrive, set out three or four blocks to help start the process. Using masking tape, outline train tracks or roads around the block area so children can build trains along the track. Four-year-olds may want to also make fences and other simple structures. Five-year-olds may enjoy creating more intricate buildings.

Bear Towns

Props: tray of small colored blocks and plastic bears

Invite children to use small blocks to build towers and walls for the little bears.

Construction Zone

Props: Legos, Duplos, magnetic blocks, Bristle Blocks, Lincoln Logs, Tinker Toys, and nesting blocks

Invite children to use commercial construction blocks for creative play. Encourage children to use nesting blocks to build skyscrapers, trains, towers, and so on.

. . . .

Let's Cook

Edible Constructions

- peanut butter
- plastic spoons
- pretzels
- cereal
- paper plates

Give each child a spoonful of peanut butter, some pretzels, and some cereal on a paper plate. Invite children to build a tower, wall, or sculpture using the edible building blocks. Then invite children to eat their creations.

Delightful Dolls

Let's Look

Wrap a doll in a gift box. Pass the box around and invite children to guess what might be inside. Then open the box and take out the doll. Give each child a turn holding the doll. Invite each child to bring a favorite doll or soft toy from home. Give children opportunities to introduce their dolls. Prepare paper award ribbons and present one to each child. Give awards for the furriest, tallest, and softest doll or toy.

Let's Talk

- What is a doll?
- How are dolls alike?
- How are dolls different?
- Do dolls have hair, eyes, noses, legs, feet?
- What is your doll's name?
- When did you get your doll?

Let's Read

Anna's Special Present by Yoriko Tsutsui

Dolls, Dolls, Dolls by Tony Tallarico

Ernest and Celestine by Gabrielle Vincent

Jamaica's Find by Juanita Havill

Mama Buy Me a China Doll by Harve Zemach

William's Doll by Charlotte Zolotow

Let's Sing and Say

Baby's Toys

Here's a ball for baby, big and soft and round.
(Make a circle with thumb and index fingers.)
Here is a baby's hammer, oh, how baby can pound.
(Pound one fist on the other.)
Here is a baby's music—clapping, clapping so!
(Clap hands.)
Here are baby's dollies, standing in a row.
(Hold up ten fingers.)
Here is baby's trumpet—toot-toot-too!
(Imitate playing a trumpet.)
Here's the way the baby plays peek-a-boo.
(Cover face and open fingers to peek out.)
Here's a big umbrella to keep baby dry.
(Hold hands up forming an umbrella.)
Here's the way baby goes a-lullabye.
(Make rocking motions with hands.)

Rag Doll

Let's play rag doll, let's not make a sound.
(Put finger to lips and say "Shh.")
Fling your legs and body loosely around.
(Move body in a limp motion.)
Fling your arms and your feet,
(Fling arms and feet.)
And let your head go free.
(Dangle head.)
Be the raggiest rag doll that you ever did see.
(Flop body loosely.)

Let's Move

Dolls

Invite children to move around the room like stiff rubber dolls and then like limp rag dolls. Children can move their "doll" heads and arms.

Let's Make

Doll Blankets

- old bed sheet

- pinking shears (for teacher use only)

- tape

- fabric crayons or markers

Use pinking shears to cut an old bed sheet into 18" squares. Tape these squares to the table and invite children to decorate them using fabric crayons or markers. Encourage children to use their homemade doll blankets in the play area.

Baby Doll Bed

- small cardboard boxes (one per child)

- wooden spools

- wood scraps or tongue depressors

- tempera paint

- paintbrushes

- glue

Invite children to paint and decorate a box to make doll beds. Children can glue wood scraps or tongue depressors to the sides or glue them to the heads of the beds to make headboards. Encourage children to glue wooden spools underneath the boxes for bed legs.

Let's Play

Newborn Nursery

Props: baby dolls, cardboard boxes, white shirts, plastic bottles, diapers, cotton swabs, baby scale, and a rocking chair

Make individual beds out of small cardboard boxes. Invite children to wear white shirts while they diaper, feed, care for, and rock the babies.

Let's Cook

Baby Doll Food

- bananas (1/2 per child)
- margarine tubs
- banana pudding mix (instant)
- low-fat milk
- small jars (one per child)
- spoons and forks

In small groups, invite children to mash the bananas in margarine tubs and set aside. Place 2 tablespoons of instant pudding in a jar for each child. Add milk until the jars are about 3/4 full. Put lids on the jars and secure them tightly. Invite children to shake their jars until pudding is firm. Children can then add some mashed bananas and enjoy their treats.

High-Flying Kites

Let's Look

Hang a colorful kite over the circle time area. Suspend it low enough so that children can see its design and construction. Include a long tail on the kite and hang it so that a portion almost touches the rug area. Display a wind-up reel for the kite's string, if possible.

Let's Talk

- What is a kite?

- What can you do with a kite?

- How are kites made?

- Why do kites need string?

- Why do kites need tails?

- Have you ever flown a kite?

Let's Read

Amy Loves the Wind by Julia Hoban

Come to the Meadow by Anna Grossnickle Hines

Curious George Flies a Kite by H.A. Rey

Do Not Disturb by Nancy Tafuri

Gilberto and the Wind by Marie Hall Ets

Kites Catch the Wind: All About Kites by Gail Gibbons

Mirandy and Brother Wind by Patricia C. McKissack

The Wind Blew by Pat Hutchins

Let's Sing and Say

My New Red Kite

Up in the sky goes my new red kite,
(Move hands up like a kite.)
Down it dives in the wind.
(Move hands down.)
Now it twists and turns around,
(Twist and turn hand.)
Then goes back up again.
(Move hand up again.)

My Kite

(Tune: "Here We Go 'Round the Mulberry Bush")
I have a kite that is blue and green,
Blue and green, blue and green.
I have a kite that is blue and green,
And it has a long, long tail.

On windy days, I fly my kite,
Fly my kite, fly my kite.
On windy days, I fly my kite,
High up in the sky.

My Kite Flies Over the Ocean

(Tune: "My Bonnie")
My kite flies over the ocean.
My kite flies over the sea.
My kite flies over the ocean.
Oh, bring back my kite to me.

Refrain:
Bring back, bring back,
Oh, bring back my kite to me, to me.
Bring back, bring back,
Oh, bring back my kite to me.

My kite flies over the meadow.
My kite flies over the trees.
My kite flies over the meadow.
Oh, bring back my kite to me.
(Repeat the refrain.)

Four Frisky Kites

Four frisky kites dancing by a tree—
One got caught, and then there were three.
Three frisky kites of yellow and blue—
One got caught, and then there were two.
Two frisky kites flying towards the sun—
One got caught, and then there was one.
One frisky kite left flying in the sky—
The kite string broke, so I waved goodbye.

The Little Kite

There was a little kite,
With a long, long tail.
*(Swoop hand down
to indicate a tail.)*
It flew over the meadow,
It flew over the trail.
(Imitate flying with hand.)
It swooped down low,
(Dip hand down.)
And it sailed up high.
(Raise hand over the head.)
It flew so high,
That it tickled the sky.
*(Reach both hands up
as if tickling the sky.)*

A Kite

I often sit and wish that I
Could be a kite up in the sky,
And ride upon the breeze and go
Whichever way I chanced to blow.

Let's Move

Kites

Give each child a paper ribbon streamer. Play music and lead the children in twisting and turning like kites in the wind. Invite children to pretend they are kites blowing in a gentle breeze or bouncing in a gusty wind. When the music stops, encourage children to gently glide down to the floor. Discuss other ways that kites might move in a wind storm, in the rain, or tied to a sailboat. (Caution children about the dangers of flying kites near power lines.)

Let's Make

Tube Kites

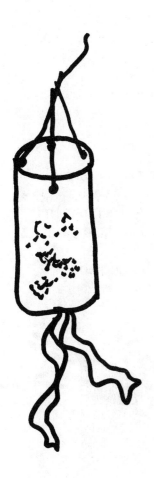

- construction paper (red, purple, yellow)
- scissors
- tempera paint (green, pink, blue, orange)
- shallow plastic tubs
- sponges
- stapler
- hole punch
- yarn
- crepe paper

Cut construction paper into rectangles of various sizes (8" x 12" or 12" x 18", for example) and give one to each child. Tear or cut a sponge into several small pieces. Place the paints in shallow plastic tubs. Invite children to dip the sponges in the paint and make prints with the sponges on their papers. When the paintings are dry, fold the paintings into cylinders and staple at each end. Punch holes in the top rim and thread with colored yarn. Attach one 18" piece of yarn to the top strings. Children can add crepe-paper streamers for tails. Encourage children to take the finished kites outside and run with them in the wind.

Kite Quilt

- butcher paper
- construction paper
- scissors
- glue

Help children cut construction paper into various kite shapes. Invite children to glue the shapes on a large piece of butcher paper to make a colorful kite quilt design.

Bag Kites

- small white paper bags (one per child)
- markers or crayons
- scissors
- hole punch
- yarn
- crepe-paper streamers

Give each child a paper bag. Invite children to draw lines and dots all over their bags. Open the bags up and cut an oval in the bottom of each bag. Then punch a hole in each corner of the bag's bottom. Thread yarn through the holes forming two triangular handles. Attach an 18" piece of yarn to the handles and add streamers to the top.

Let's Play

Flying Kites

Props: kites

Give children an opportunity to go outside in an open space and fly kites.

Blowin' in the Wind

Props: pinwheels, sailboats, wind chimes, flags, and paper airplanes

Set up a learning center of toys that move in the wind. Encourage children to experiment with the wind toys.

Music

Props: empty bottles, combs, tissue paper, cardboard tubes, waxed paper, and rubberbands

If possible, invite a musician to visit your classroom and demonstrate ways he or she makes music by blowing through a mouthpiece or reed. Let children examine the mouthpieces. Encourage children to make their own instruments with the props listed. Children can blow across the tops of empty bottles or blow through combs covered with tissue paper. Or, children can cover the ends of cardboard tubes with waxed paper and create sounds by blowing.

Let's Cook

Cheesy Apple Kitewiches

- bread
- cookie cutters
- pimento cheese spread
- fruits and vegetables (thinly sliced)
- spaghetti (cooked)
- paper plates
- plastic knives

Invite children to cut kite shapes from bread slices using cookie cutters. Have children cover their kite shapes with cheese spread. Then encourage children to use a spaghetti noodle for a kite tail and decorate the rest of the kite with fruit and vegetable slices. Invite children to enjoy their kitewiches.

Bouncing Balls

Let's Look

Place a collection of balls (tennis balls, ping-pong balls, golf balls, soft rubber balls, foam balls, small rubber footballs) in a cloth bag. Pass the bag around the circle and invite children to hold and feel the different balls.

Let's Talk

- Are balls toys?
- How do balls move?
- What can you do with balls?
- What shape are balls?
- Do you have a ball? What kind?

Let's Read

The Ball Bounced by Nancy Tafuri

Balloonia by Audrey Wood

Beach Ball by Peter Sis

Let's Play Ball, Ned by Pam Hope-Zinnemann

Look Around: A Book About Shapes by Leonard E. Fisher

Toys by Sara Lynn

Yellow Ball by Molly Bang

Let's Sing and Say

Here's a Ball

Here's a ball, I throw it high.
Look, it almost touched the sky.
(Imitate throwing the ball up.)
Now I bounce it on the ground,
Boom, boom, boom, boom,
what a sound.
(Imitate bouncing a ball.)
Now I roll it gently so.
(Imitate rolling a ball.)
Watch, let's see where it will go.
(Place hand across eyebrows, looking.)

Here Is a Ball

(Tune: "Lazy Mary, Will You Get Up?")
Here is a ball all shiny and blue,
(Make a ball with hands.)
Roll it to me and I'll roll it to you.
(Pretend to roll a ball.)
Here is a ball all shiny and black,
(Make a ball with hands.)
Bounce it once and give it back.
(Pretend to bounce a ball.)
Here is a ball all shiny and red,
(Make a ball with hands.)
Throw it high above your head.
(Pretend to throw a ball.)
Here is a ball all shiny and brown,
(Make a ball with hands.)
It's time to stop and put it down.
(Pretend to place the ball on the floor.)

Bounce the Ball

(Tune: "Row, Row, Row Your Boat")
Bounce, bounce, bounce your ball,
Bounce it very high.
Bounce it on the ceiling,
Bounce it to the sky.

Roll, roll, roll your ball,
Roll it on the floor.
Roll it very slowly,
Roll it out the door.

Throw, throw, throw your ball,
Throw it to a friend.
When your friend catches it,
Do it all again.

Counting Balls

Here's a ball.
*(Put thumb and index finger
together to form a small circle.)*
Here's a ball.
*(Put hands together,
touching thumbs and fingers.)*
And here's a great big ball I see.
(Make a circle with arms.)
Are you ready?
Shall, we count them?
One, two, three!
(Remake each size ball.)

Let's Move

Bouncing Balls

Give each child a ball. Invite children to roll, bounce, toss, and kick their balls around. Use a large beach ball or cage ball for group play. Closely supervise this activity.

Let's Make

Frisbee Art

- construction paper
- scissors
- frisbees
- tempera paint (thin)
- eyedroppers
- collection of balls (golf, rubber, tennis)
- tongs

Cut construction-paper circles to fit inside the rim of a frisbee. Help the children use an eyedropper to drop several colors of paint onto the papers. Then have children place balls on the papers and roll the balls around in the frisbees to spread the paint drops. Remove the balls with metal tongs. Help children remove the colorfully designed papers from the frisbees to dry.

Beautiful Balls

- balloons (one per child)
- glue
- paper cups
- yarn
- ribbon

Give each child a blown-up balloon, a cup of diluted glue, and yarn strips of various colors. Invite children to dip yarn in the glue and place it around the balloon. After the yarn designs dry, pop the balloons. Hang the beautiful string balls with ribbon and display in the classroom.

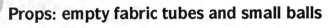

Let's Play

Balls and Tubes

Props: empty fabric tubes and small balls

Invite children to roll small balls through the cardboard tubes. Encourage children to place the tubes at different heights and angles.

Ramps

Props: wooden blocks, variety of balls, and masking tape

Invite children to help set up several ramps using various sizes of blocks. Encourage children to predict which balls will roll the farthest down the ramps. Invite children to place the balls at the top of the ramps and release the balls at the same time. Watch where each ball stops and mark the place with masking tape. Encourage children to continue experimenting with ramps at different heights and angles.

Water Fun

Props: water table, ping-pong balls, and nerf balls

Invite children to experiment with ping-pong and nerf balls at the water table. Children can see which will sink and which will float.

Classification

Props: variety of balls (beach balls, soccer balls, tennis balls, basketballs, ping-pong balls)

Encourage children to sort and classify the balls and to arrange them by size. Or, arrange the balls by the distance they roll with a single push.

Blow Up the Balls

Props: air pump and inflatable balls

Give children an opportunity to use an air pump to blow up some balls.

Let's Cook

Chunky Cheese Balls

- 6 oz cream cheese
- 1 cup grated cheddar cheese
- 1/4 cup pineapple bits
- 1/4 cup crushed walnuts
- plastic knives
- crackers
- waxed paper

Give children small amounts of cream cheese, shredded cheddar cheese, pineapple bits, and crushed walnuts. Invite children to mix and roll the mixture on waxed paper to form balls. Serve on paper plates. Encourage children to spread the mixture on crackers.

General Guidelines for Early-Childhood Programs

1. Make each child's preschool experience positive and enjoyable by offering continued acceptance in a loving, nurturing environment.

2. Provide a safe environment in which children freely play and explore.

3. Encourage positive feelings about self, family, and the child's home environment by providing multicultural and nonsexist materials and experiences.

4. Encourage young children's thinking, investigating, and problem-solving abilities by offering a rich variety of activities and materials that give children developmentally appropriate choices.

5. Plan a curriculum that emphasizes learning by doing with play as the primary teaching vehicle.

6. Observe each child carefully and when appropriate encourage learning by asking questions, offering suggestions, providing more challenging materials, or encouraging participation in specific activities.

7. Recognize that young children may choose to practice newly acquired skills over and over, gradually extending to more complex skills.

8. Plan daily routines that help children develop a sense of trust and security. Include opportunities for individual and group interacting.

9. Foster awareness of the environment, our responsibility to it, and the changes that can and do occur.

10. Provide opportunities to build on prior knowledge and encourage children to take risks, solve their own problems, and make decisions.

11. Offer a variety of experiences, materials, and equipment to expand children's abilities to use small and large muscles in many ways.

12. Encourage children to share thoughts, feelings, and experiences in a variety of ways.

13. Help children explore ways of dealing with conflicts as they begin to share, cooperate, and live in harmony with others.

14. Recognize that parents are young children's first and foremost teachers and should be actively involved in learning and teaching.

15. Focus on children's strengths and not their weaknesses. Celebrate accomplishments.

16. Tailor your program to meet the specific needs of the children, rather than expecting the children to adjust to the demands of a specific program.

First Time Circle Time

Art Recipes

Bubble Solution

- 3 cups water
- 1 cup liquid soap
- 1 Tbsp sugar

Mix the ingredients well. Use this solution in science experiments and related activities.

Playdough

- 2 cups flour
- 1/2 cup salt
- 1 Tbsp alum
- 1 1/2 cups water
- 1 Tbsp cooking oil
- food coloring (optional)

Bring the water to a boil. Add the cooking oil and food coloring. Then add the dry ingredients. Mix and knead the mixture until smooth. Store the playdough in a plastic bag or container in the refrigerator.

Collage Paste

- 1 cup flour
- 1 cup water
- 2 cups boiling water
- 1 tsp alum
- 1 tsp oil of wintergreen

Mix the flour into 1 cup water. Slowly add 2 cups boiling water. Cook in a double boiler over low heat until smooth. Then add the alum and oil of wintergreen and cook the mixture. Store the paste in a closed container in a cool place.

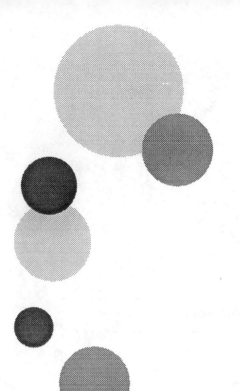

Fingerpaint #1

- 2 Tbsp sugar
- 2 cups cold water
- 1/2 cup cornstarch
- food coloring

Mix the sugar and cornstarch. Slowly add the water and cook over low heat, stirring constantly until blended. Divide the mixture into portions and add the desired food coloring.

Fingerpaint #2

- 3 cups water
- 1 cup wallpaper-paste powder
- food coloring
- 1 cup salt (optional)

Stir the wallpaper-paste powder into the water. Divide the mixture into portions and add food coloring as desired. Add 1 cup salt to the mixture for a different tactile sensation.

Clay #1

- 4 cups flour
- 1 1/2 cups water
- 1 cup salt
- food coloring (optional)

Mix all the ingredients in a bowl. Knead the clay for 10 minutes. Then roll the clay 1/4" thick and cut the clay with cookie cutters or mold the clay into various shapes.

Clay #2

- 1 cup salt
- 1/2 cup cornstarch
- 1/2 cup boiling water
- food coloring (optional)

Heat all the ingredients, stirring constantly until the mixture is too thick to stir. Cool and knead the clay until smooth. Then mold the clay into desired shapes.

Making Props

Mystery Box
- shoebox
- scissors
- wrapping paper
- tape

Cut a 3" hole in one end of a shoebox. Cover the lid and bottom of the box with wrapping paper separately, so the lid can be removed.

Drawstring Bag
- 1/2 yard lightweight fabric
- cotton cord
- thread
- pinking shears
- pins
- sewing machine
- iron

Using pinking shears, cut fabric into 6" x 18" rectangles. Fold the rectangles in half lengthwise (right sides together) to form 6" x 9" bags. Iron along the fold. Open flat with right side of fabric down. Fold down 1/4" on each end. Iron and stitch. Fold down a 1" casing on each hemmed end. Iron and stitch casing. Again, fold the fabric with right sides together and pin the sides. Stitch the sides, stopping at the casing. Turn right side out and iron. Thread a cord through the casing and knot at one end.

Sock Puppets
- socks
- glue
- decorating materials (yarn, ribbon, button, chenille stems, felt)
- scissors

Using decorating materials, add facial features and other details to the socks to make puppet faces.

Paper-Plate Puppets

- paper plates
- glue
- tongue depressor, popsicle sticks, or paint paddle sticks
- crayons or markers
- yarn
- felt
- construction paper

Glue a tongue depressor or popsicle stick between two paper plates for a puppet handle. Add facial features and other details to both sides of the plate puppet. For example, draw a happy face on one side and a sad face on the other. Or, create animal puppets.

Necklace Flannelboard

- cardboard
- scissors
- ribbon
- felt
- glue

Cover a 5" x 8" cardboard rectangle with felt. Attach a 1-inch wide ribbon to each side so the ribbon is long enough to tie around a teacher's neck.

Storytime Apron

- baker's apron
- permanent markers
- cookie cutters
- acrylic paint

Draw designs on an apron using permanent markers. Or, dip cookie cutters in acrylic paint and make prints on the apron. It is useful if the apron has a pocket. Put a small toy or object in the pocket to introduce a story or concept.

Storytime Hat

- straw hat
- glue
- decorations (flowers, ribbon, toy animals)

Glue decorations or small toy animals to the brim and crown of a straw hat.

The Bigger Circle - Saving the Earth

Recycling from A - Z

Children should be made aware at an early age that they are members of a larger community. Provide experiences that teach children to be responsible for making the world a better place. Once you and your students become committed to recycling, there are endless possibilities for conserving resources. For example, encourage the support of families in helping with year-round gardening projects that include composting. Encourage children to recycle toys, clothing, and books. Invite parents to help organize a book and toy exchange or sponsor a used-clothing sale or swap. Model conservation by using recyclable materials for classroom projects. Save the items listed on pages 272-283 from A-Z.

Items

Uses

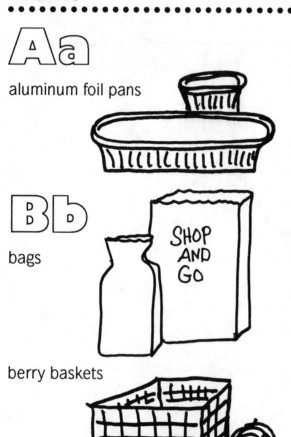

Aa
aluminum foil pans

- containers for paint and collage items

Bb
bags

- cut them apart for art paper or decorate them for puppets or masks

berry baskets

- weave to make colorful baskets
- line with foil, fill with soil, and plant seeds
- use to hold crayons or collage materials
- use as sieves in sand and water tables

boxes

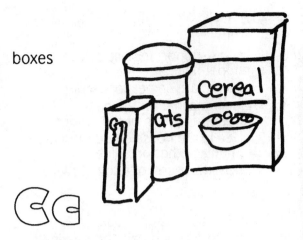

- cut and use for dramatic-play props
- use for sculptures
- use to store classroom equipment
- tape shut and use for classroom building blocks
- decorate as a treasure or mystery box

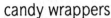

candy wrappers

- add to collage box
- use foil wrappers for decoration

cloth

- cut and glue on sock puppets
- make clothes for puppets
- spread on floor for block play
- wrap around head or body for costumes
- make drawstring bags

cotton balls

- add to collage box

corrugated paper from cookies and candies

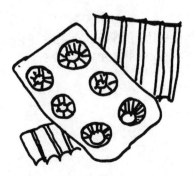

- add to collage box
- add to easel for interesting painting surfaces
- use in paper weavings

clothespins

- use as support for salt-clay puppet heads
- use in math games for sorting
- glue a magnet on the back and use for a refrigerator memo holder
- place in the house center and use to hang clothes on a line
- use as the body of a toy airplane

clothes

- add to the costume box
- save to sort and hang on the line
- collect for others who could use them

Dd

dirt

Potting Soil

- use in collages
- use for planting or gardening projects

Ee

egg cartons

eggs
eggs

- use to hold small office supplies
- cut up for collages
- fill with paints for cotton-swab painting

eggshells

- plant seeds in shell halves
- color and crush for collages

First Time Circle Time

envelopes

- use at writing center

eyedroppers

- use for color experiments and dropper art

Ff

fast-food containers

- use for storage
- cut up for collages
- use as bases for art projects

film canisters

- fill with different objects for sound canisters

flowers

- replant root cuttings
- press and use to decorage gifts
- save the seeds, dry, and replant

Gg

gloves

- use for puppets
- glue to the back of flannelboard shapes

Hh

hole punch dots

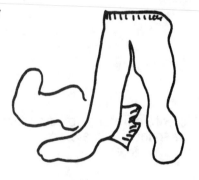

- add to collage box
- place near easel to add to wet paintings

hosiery

- cut up and stuff to make soft sculptures
- stretch over wire hangers for masks

Ii

icing containers

- use for storage
- use to make drums

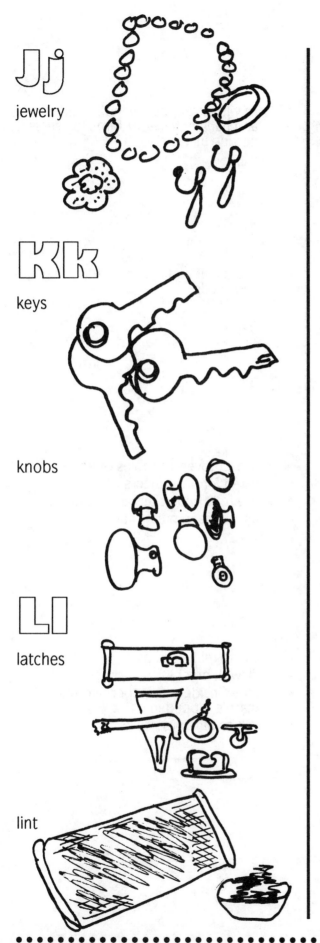

Jj
jewelry

- add to art box for special gift making
- put in costume trunk

Kk
keys

- add to dramatic-play prop box
- include in manipulative center for sorting

knobs

- add to woodworking area for accessories

Ll
latches

- attach to a board in the manipulative center

lint

- add to collage box

Mm

mesh bags

- fill with straw, pine needles, and string, and hang outside for birds to use as nesting materials

milk cartons

- cut in half and use to hold potting soil and seeds

Nn

newspapers

- use to cover art tables or easels
- shred for art projects
- use to to wipe classroom windows
- use to make paper hats and boats

oatmeal containers

- use to make drums
- fill with brushes for storage
- cover inside with paper and roll a marble dipped in paint
- use as building blocks

Pp

packing materials

- use for storage
- add to collage box

paper

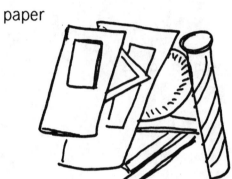

- use for drawing and writing
- use for easel painting
- cut and use for collages

plastic containers

- use to make gifts
- use to hold paint

Qq

quart-size containers with lids

- fill with water or soil for observation projects
- punch holes in lids to make insect homes

Rr

rubberbands

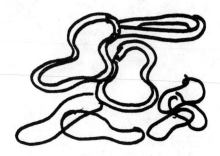

- use with geoboards

Ss

shoe-polish bottles

- refill with paint for easel painting

socks

- decorate for puppets
- fill with fiberfill and use for stitchery projects
- fill with dried beans and tie off tops to make beanbags

styrofoam containers

- tear and glue to collage pictures
- use for making hats

Tt

tires

- fill with dirt for gardening

tissue paper

- add to collage box

Uu

umbrellas

- hang over circle area
- use the frame only to hang wet paintings

upholstery samples

- add to collage box

Vv

valentines

- place in literacy center
- cut and use in collages

wallpaper

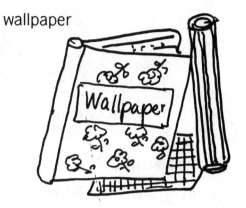

- add to collage box
- cut and glue to boxes for gifts
- use for painting

XxYyZz

yarn

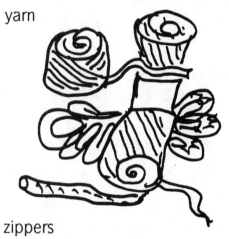

- make puppet hair

zippers

- place in the manipulative center

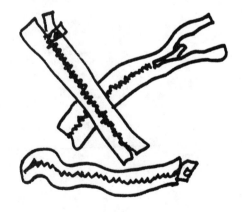

Other Ways to Recycle and Save Energy

- Always carry a litter bag with you on field trips.

- Avoid using household chemicals for classroom cleaning. Substitute baking soda for powdered cleansers and vinegar and water for bleach.

- Use paper products or reusable plastic.

- Conserve on paper by cutting napkins in fourths and paper towels in half.

- Carry a cloth bag to the grocery store instead of using paper or plastic.

- Recycle food scraps and avoid excessive use of food products in art projects.

- Make trash collectors from cereal boxes. Form trash patrols to regularly pick up litter left around the school grounds.

- Turn out lights when you leave a room.

Resources and Recommended Reading

Ames, Louise Bates. *Your Three Year Old: Friend or Enemy*. New York: Dell Publishing, 1976.

Ames, Louise Bates, et al. *The Gesell Institute's Child from One to Six*. New York: Harper & Row, 1979.

Bos, Beverly. *Don't Move the Muffin Tins*. Roseville, CA: Turn-the-Page-Press, 1982.

Bredekamp, Sue (editor). *Developmentally Appropriate Practice*. Washington, DC: National Association for the Education of Young Children, 1987.

Brittain, W.L. *Creativity, Art and the Young Child*. New York: Macmillan Publishing, 1979.

Cherry, Clare. *Creative Movement for the Developing Child: A Nursery School Handbook for Non-Musicians*. Carthage, IL: Fearon Teacher Aids, 1971.

Dodge, Diane Trister. *The Creative Curriculum for Early Childhood*. Washington, DC: Teaching Strategies, Inc., 1991.

Elkind, David. *Miseducation—Preschoolers at Risk*. New York: Knopf, 1987.

Flemming, Bonnie Mack. *Resources for Creative Teaching in Early Childhood Education*. New York: Harcourt Brace Jovanovich, 1977.

Glazer, Tom. *Eye Winker, Tom Tinker, Chin Chopper: Fifty Musical Fingerplays*. Garden City, NY: Doubleday, 1973.

Grayson, Marion F. *Let's Do Fingerplays.* New York: David McKay, 1960.

Pulaski, Mary Ann. *Understanding Piaget*. New York: Harper & Row, 1971.

Schickendanz, Judith A. *More Than ABC's: The Early Stages of Reading and Writing*. Washington, DC: National Association for the Education of Young Children, 1983.

Strickland, Dorothy S. and Lesley Mandel Morrow. *Emerging Literacy: Young Children Learn to Read and Write*. Newark, DE: International Reading Association, 1989.

Trelease, Jim. *The Read-Aloud Handbook*. Baltimore, MD: Penguin Books, 1982.

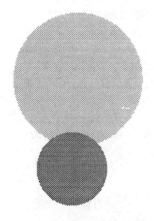

About the Authors

Cynthia Holley has over 20 years of experience teaching in preschool, kindergarten, and special education classrooms. She holds a Master's Degree in Early Childhood Education and Special Education. She has served as a consultant to special education and early childhood education programs in the United States and Europe. Cynthia is also the author of *Holiday Stories, Bilingual Babies, Every Day in Every Way* and *Resources for Every Day in Every Way*.

Jane Walkup is a graduate of George Peabody College of Vanderbilt University. She has a degree in Elementary Education with an emphasis in Early Childhood Education. Jane has taught at Queen's College and Central Piedmont Community College. She has worked in both public and private preschools and kindergartens. She is the former director of the Early Learning Center at Queen's College and Today's Child, a creative arts center in Charlotte, North Carolina.

Both authors conduct workshops for early childhood educators in North Carolina and throughout the United States.